CONTENTS

Illustrations

Introduction

The Relevance of Piracy

Until recently, the phrase *maritime piracy* conjured up romanticized caricatures of seventeenth and eighteenth century Caribbean pirates enshrined in popular media. Far from being limited to a single era or geographic area, though, maritime piracy is a phenomenon that has existed almost as long as ships have plied the world's oceans. Piracy near Somalia is merely the latest episode to attract the world's attention. The contemporary rash of piracy remains a pressing problem. Events like the 7 April 2009 kidnapping of Captain Richard Phillips, the first American citizen held by foreign pirates since 1903, may accelerate and expand the visible response by US military forces.[1] Inevitable future changes aside, the US military response to piracy near Somalia has already unfolded as a compelling story with an interesting plot twist. During the ascendance of Somali pirates on the global stage, US policy for dealing with them changed because of actions by rival states. In simple terms, the initial US military response to piracy was isolationist. Other than a token participation in anti-piracy measures, the US diplomatic and military establishments were willing to let the response to piracy come from other countries. A visible commitment of Russian and Chinese warships to the issue of Somali piracy changed this situation.

This thesis argues that the change in US policy that led to increased intervention near Somalia marks a shift along an isolationist-interventionist foreign policy spectrum. The change is the result of two international relations (IR) phenomena colliding. The first phenomenon is a tendency toward isolationism, a result of the United States' unique strategic culture. The second phenomenon is an ineluctable US response to visible military activity by its rivals in areas where the United States anticipates a prevailing security influence. The initial, isolationist tendency arose from cultural roots; national

---

[1] Chip Cummins, Louise Radnofsky, and Phillip Shishkin, "US Ship Repels Pirates," *The Wall Street Journal*, 9 April 2009. Sam Cho, a Chinese businessperson who was "the richest Chinaman in Hawaii," was captured by and subsequently rescued from pirates on the Canton River in China. The newspaper account highlights his political connections, noting that he received his US citizenship because of close ties to Hawaiian leadership when it became a US territory. A US warship fought off his captors in China. See "Rescued from Pirates: Sam Cho, Wealthy Honolulu Chinaman and American Citizen, Was Captured on the Canton River," *The New York Times*, 22 July 1903.

1

will and choice shaped it. The latter, interventionist proclivity stemmed from national instincts awakened when rivals challenged US hegemony; it conflicted with the earlier conscious national choice, but proved impossible to resist.

This thesis is *not* a discussion of how to stop the scourge of piracy emanating from Somalia. Put simply, Somali piracy stems from Somalia's status of "the world's most utterly failed state."[2] The country is a shambles of competing tribal-based rivalries, militant Islamic fundamentalism, and thug-like warlords. While there are some recognizable semblances of control in parts of the nation that collapsed in the early 1990s, there is not even a shell of central control, and much of the country lives in complete anarchy. Most of the reason for piracy's success is that it brings economic wealth and a degree of structure to the coastal towns, home to individuals with the maritime expertise required for them to make a living as pirates. Expert opinions on the exact mechanics for stopping or slowing Somali piracy differ, but all find common ground in addressing the problem of shore-based anarchy. This discussion pertains to US and international military response *at sea* to the problem of Somali piracy.

This study will focus only on piracy in those waters proximate to the Somali coast. In 2000, an area a few dozen miles wide in the Gulf of Aden and the Indian Ocean was susceptible to piracy. Nevertheless, the increasing temerity of pirates in the area has extended this range beyond 500 nautical miles from Somali territory.[3] Piracy in Africa is not limited to Somalia; until 2005, the western waters near Nigeria and the Gulf of Guinea were the most likely place for African pirate attacks. While piracy plagues the rest of the world, including the Far East—the Straits of Malacca and the Hong Kong-Luzon-Hainan (HLH) Triangle get special attention from anti-piracy organizations— several qualitative and quantitative differences exist between these other areas and the Somali coast. In the Far East, and to a lesser extent, western Africa, piracy is a serious and often dangerous nuisance, but one that is under control because of regional and international cooperation. In contrast, piracy near and originating from the Horn of Africa has exploded, exhibiting unbounded growth in recent years. The business model of Somali pirates is unique. In the Far East, a typical pirate attack robs ships of cash and

---

[2] "The World's Most Utterly Failed State," *The Economist*, 4 October 2008, 49.
[3] Peter Chalk, (RAND Corporation), interview by author, 30 January 2009

maritime equipment that pirates can resell. An average take is worth $5,000, and attacks are over in a few minutes or a few hours. In the Somali ransom-based approach, pirates often hold ships for months, and ransoms routinely reach or exceed $1 million.

Not only is Somali piracy unique in terms of expense, it occurs there more frequently than any other place on the globe. Pirate attacks off the Somali coast accelerated dramatically after 2003, culminating in a staggering increase in 2008. Over 110 incidents of piracy plagued the Gulf of Aden and Indian Ocean in 2008—more than one third of all pirate attacks worldwide.[4] By demanding large ransoms in exchange for the safe return of crews and vessels, Somalis practiced a form of piracy uncommon in other areas of the world. Pirates received over $100 million in ransom money, making by far the single largest economic contribution to the fractured fiefdoms that make up present-day Somalia. Because ships passing through the Suez Canal must traverse the waters threatened by Somali pirates, this brand of modern piracy has unnerved the world's merchant mariners and has influenced shipping patterns. Subsequently, piracy attracted the attention of a wide range of nations who are also major world powers.

Following the introduction of Russian and Chinese warships, there was a palpable shift in US military and diplomatic response. Not content to encourage from the sidelines, the United States exhibited a growing desire for a leadership role in the emerging Western anti-piracy effort. US policy makers responded in two ways. The first involved diplomatic overtures in the United Nations. The second, more immediately visible, was in the form of military commitment. The US Navy stood up a dedicated anti-piracy task force and reclaimed the lead of that body from its coalition partners. In the course of overcoming an aversion to apprehending pirates because of international law concerns, diplomatic efforts created an agreement with Kenya that put US military personnel in the business of not only deterring pirate attacks, but also arresting pirates and delivering them for prosecution. Strong rhetoric from US admirals addressing the situation announced a revived US effort.

---

[4] "French Navy Foils Somali Pirate Attack," *AFP* (27 January 2009), http://www.google.com/hostednews/afp/article/ALeqM5iniI4Hpem2JKcN1RtzJU5KGA9pWw (accessed 28 January 2009).

Important Definitions

Analyzing the development of US policy from a constructivist viewpoint (strategic culture), as well as a determinist outlook (structural realism), creates stark dichotomies between the desires of security elites and the responsibilities of a unitary superpower. Chapter 3 details these dichotomies, but it is useful in this thesis to define core terms that will frame the subsequent argument. *Interventionism* in this thesis refers to a nation's willingness to involve itself in the affairs of another. The context of this study gives the most weight to military intervention, although a limited amount of political intervention occurred to make the military variety legitimate and palatable to the international community. *Isolationism* is the abstention from alliances and other international political bodies. This thesis argues that intervention and isolation are two extremes on a spectrum that can explain the reasons for US military commitment to combating piracy near Somalia. Because the spectrum of concern deals with a narrow issue (that is, piracy near Somalia), the terms serve to describe this specific behavior without touching on other issues. For example, saying that US policy was isolationist in this case does not imply the United States withdrew from its NATO obligations or suspended its cooperation with the World Trade Organization (WTO)—the use of the terms extends to piracy alone.

The term *strategic culture* also requires some explanation. While strategic culture appears frequently as a term of art in IR literature, it has enough elasticity to be almost meaningless. To provide suitable limits, this thesis adopts the approach of Alan Macmillan and Ken Booth, who define strategic culture as "a nation's traditions, values, attitudes, patterns of behavior, habits, symbols, achievements and particular ways of adapting to the environment and solving problems with respect to the threat or use of force."[5] This definition includes many facets of culture, but its emphasis on force helps bound the discussion of piracy, as it ignores introspective—and distracting—aspects of strategic culture and focuses on a cultural artifact (force or the threat of force) that is easier to observe.

---

[5] Alan Macmillan and Ken Booth, "Appendix: Strategic Culture–Framework for Analysis," in *Strategic Cultures in the Asia-Pacific Region*, ed. Ken Booth and Russell Trood (New York: St. Martin's Press, 1999), 363.

A Larger Problem

Examining the US military response to piracy is to examine a subset of a larger problem. A succinct statement of the problem asks, "*Is the United States doing what it must to retain its power and influence as the world's hegemon?*" This thesis concludes that, with respect to Somali piracy, the United States has responded adequately. Security elites, however, did not adequately consider and calculate the initial US response to piracy; US actions were instead an automatic, isolationist response to a distasteful problem. Only after the willingness of rivals to fill the leadership abdicated by the United States became apparent did an appropriate US response follow, coming in answer to a kind of strategic wakeup call.

What strategic importance does piracy have? Admittedly, for all the startling figures and stories arising from it, Somali piracy is a small event on the world's stage. Nevertheless, piracy in general and the response of leading countries to it has defined hegemons and superpowers throughout recorded history. In essence, an ability and a willingness to prevent piracy in areas where it flourishes signals the presence of a hegemon. Inability to fight piracy with success signals a waning power, or at least defines a part of the world as falling outside a hegemon's influence. As David Myers has framed the matter, "Strategic responses to threats against regional hegemony are long term."[6] He goes on to differentiate between actions designed to maintain long term advantage, which are strategic, and actions designed to respond to relatively minor situations while pursuing larger goals. This thesis argues that piracy off Africa's east coast is a strategic matter for the United States. It argues that the explosion of piracy there was not merely an international inconvenience; the United States could not afford a lackadaisical response to it. Rather, East African piracy is a strategic problem in its own right, and the US military response reveals much about US willingness to pursue hegemonic power. The fact that there was discontinuity between the nation's initial cultural response and its later structural response reveals a degree of uncertainty in the organs of IR decision-making. The United States must resolve this internal conflict or it risks seeing its position of world leadership erode by a commensurate amount.

---

[6] David J. Myers, "Threat Perception and Strategic Response of the Regional Hegemons: A Conceptual Overview," in *Regional Hegemons: Threat Perception and Strategic Response*, ed. David J. Myers (Boulder, CO: Westview Press, Inc., 1991), 23.

This thesis uses piracy to make the case that the US should accept and embrace responsibility for global security. The argument proceeds with a description of piracy, a listing of competing theoretical frameworks for its analysis, and an examination of piracy within those frameworks. In concluding that the United States stumbled in its initial response to piracy, unmasking a degree of uncharacteristic national uncertainty about US power, the thesis arrives at these preliminary conclusions. First, the US had an opportunity to respond unilaterally to piracy—doing this would be consistent with historic US policy toward piracy. Second, the US did not seize this leadership opportunity, preferring to encourage involvement by its close allies, and even permitting its rivals to take a prominent place in battling the problem. Third, after standing by for a period of time that witnessed an explosion in the scope and audacity of piracy near the Horn of Africa, the US seized a greater leadership role. In leading this anti-piracy charge, the United States first emphasized its own unilateral commitment before returning to calls for multilateral cooperation. Behind this show of multilateralism, the overall effort was a direct response to countries that do not align with US interests, who often choose to act in spoiler roles, and who may have chosen to respond to piracy as a means of challenging US hegemony. Fourth, case-specific cultural influences shaped the US response to piracy; the response appears structured and based on both enduring and contemporary security preferences. Fifth, other actors in the international system, particularly rival states, forced the US response. Even though it attempted to construct an idealist solution to dealing with piracy, the United States' status as a major power with the capacity to act relative to its rivals determined its response.

The thesis concludes by asserting that the apparent tension between strategic culture and structural realism evident in the US response to Somali piracy is a useful way to examine many long-term strategic problems. The mechanism for resolution is acknowledgment of a specific and fundamental level of strategic culture, one that is not malleable among the hammers and anvils of contemporary elite opinions, but instead rests in fixed geo-cultural and national self-image aspects of culture. A realization emerges that when limited definitions and shortened time horizons bound a study of strategic culture, it appears to be weak and subject to structural realism. This thesis argues that, in fact, the degree to which a nation "participates" in structural realism defines acceptance of more fundamental cultural norms. Recent Somali piracy and the response of rival nations to it revealed bright lines of international behavior that elicit an ineluctable US response. The bright lines that elicit a national response of force are both structural reality as well as cultural constructs: they are tacit national preferences that endure longer than the constructs devised by security elites. Put another way, the actions that elicit a response of force from a given nation define both structural realist bounds and the deepest levels of strategic culture in that nation. Since strategic culture and structural realism are subjects that academic literature tends to isolate and separate, this paper's approach offers a way ahead for both schools to benefit from shared insights. Realizing the fundamental American strategic cultural desire for hegemony can prevent future hiccups like the one that initially characterized the US military response to piracy.

Structure

Chapter 1 provides a brief historical sketch of piracy and other maritime issues through the turn of the twenty-first century. This will serve to put Somali piracy in context with previous notable eras of pirate activity, and will provide background of the important international law issues that frame US understanding of and response to piracy. It discusses the response of world powers, including the United States, to the plague of piracy on the world's oceans. Each era of history will demonstrate that piracy exists under conditions of anarchy in places that define the effective edge of empires or hegemonic influence. Further, countries that have responded successfully to piracy have established or maintained regional or global influence. When an established power was unable to meet the challenge posed by pirates, the event signaled a declining power.

Chapter 2 continues the piracy narrative with more detail about modern Somali piracy. The chapter shows the magnitude of the problem and discusses the characteristics that make Somali piracy different from modern piracy in other geographic areas. At the same time, Somali piracy conforms to the broader characteristics of historical piracy, namely that its existence demonstrates the presence of anarchy and begs for a hegemonic power to exert stabilizing influence for the benefit of the entire international order.

Chapter 3 establishes a theoretical background, providing sketches of two ways to view piracy. The chapter describes the strategic cultural and the structural realist approaches to examining national military response. The thesis examines competing ideas within both major schools, and enumerates areas where they agree and disagree. The chapter concludes by synthesizing the two theories into a combined model. This approach provides a way to accommodate otherwise irreconcilable differences between the two theories. The chapter also points out, however, that genuine differences between strategic culture and structural realities, especially for a superpower or hegemon, may simply reflect a shifting attitude about its role in the global power structure. Chapter 3 is a generalized approach. It uses the case of Somali piracy to illustrate some points, but deliberately takes a broad view that allows applicability to several scenarios involving the potential use of military force.

Chapter 4 applies the theory from chapter 3 to the specifics of Somali piracy discussed in chapter 2. The chapter shows that an isolationist response, understood best through a lens of strategic culture, marked the initial US response to piracy. The involvement in counter-piracy efforts by Russia and China—two aspiring near-peer competitors—changed desired isolationism to forced interventionism. This chapter argues the two main points of the thesis.

The first point is that strategic culture is not a short-term construct trumped by structural realism's harsh dictates. On the contrary, US acquiescence to the dictates of structural realism reveals something more fundamental about US strategic culture. The study of strategic culture and structural realism in the context of modern maritime piracy suggests good reasons for a continued study of all types of strategic culture. Such a study demonstrates that the most important measure of a nation's strategic culture is the military commitment it finds unavoidable. The structural realist constraints a nation views as mandatory provide insight into its enduring strategic culture.

The second point is that these enduring cultural dimensions are only as strong as national will. Even with a power base big enough to act as a hegemon or a unilateral superpower, a nation that chooses to do so can lay down that mantle of power in the absence of a rival or catastrophic event wresting it away. The initial subdued US response to Somali piracy may reflect such a trend, and deserves vigorous debate if this path is the one favored by the national elites who exert the preponderance of current influence on the nation's strategic culture. This thesis argues that the desire for worldly approbation in vogue with US policy makers is a passing fancy, and that acting as apologists for US power by failing to exercise it in response to clear challenges like piracy is a poor foreign policy decision. Instead of shying away from the use of military force when the world looks to the United States to provide stabilizing leadership in the face of anarchy, the United States should embrace the responsibility so that it can continue rightfully in its role as superpower.

Chapter 1

History of Piracy

Like the pirate himself, the skull and crossbones symbol used on pirate flags has become an instantly recognizable and identifiable image—a symbol of piracy and of rebellion against authority.

—Angus Konstam, *Piracy: the Complete History*

Introduction

Piracy is predictable—it has existed since humankind took to the seas and flourishes under easily identified conditions. This chapter provides background on maritime piracy from antiquity to the first decade of the twenty-first century. The obvious conclusion from this background is that piracy is an enduring phenomenon associated with ocean-going trade; it has appeared periodically in various areas of the world. The appearance of piracy, moreover, is cyclic; it flourishes when no central government or great power enforces maritime law.[1] Nations or empires that have stopped piracy have done so by using military force to uphold laws governing behavior on the open sea. A more subtle point this chapter demonstrates is that a nation able to stop piracy from flourishing usually becomes or remains a regional hegemon or global superpower. In the obverse, the rise of piracy in the face of a superpower or hegemon signals waning power—a decline that extends beyond a nation's ability to police the high seas.

This chapter proceeds chronologically. After providing evidence of piracy's historical trends and its effects on hegemons and superpowers, the chapter concludes by

---

[1] Gosse offers four historical phases of piracy: (1) a few outlaws practice the crime, (2) pirates organize so that no ship is free from attack, (3) the pirate organization is a *de facto* state, able to make useful alliances with a legitimate state, and (4) piracy reverts to the first stage, either because the pirate organization loses a war or becomes a victorious and legitimate new state. Historically, few bouts of piracy progress through all of these stages. Philip Gosse, *The History of Piracy*, Tudor ed. (New York: Longmans, Green and Co., 1932). A more tongue-in-cheek construct posits an alternate pirate development schema: (1) cruel, criminal, charismatic historical figure, (2) swashbuckling protagonist in many forms of media, and (3) subject of caricature and marketing. See David Montgomery, "Pillage People: Until Their Legacy Becomes a Punch Line, Somali Pirates Sail Scary Cultural Seas," *The Washington Post*, 6 December 2008, C1.

describing piracy at the beginning of the twenty-first century. In many parts of the world, piracy remained a dangerous threat to thousands of ships each year, but effective international response by stable nations limited the economic scourge of piracy and assuaged international concern about it. This description contrasts with the description in chapter 2 of Somali piracy: piracy in Somalia exploded in a region unable to respond, and increasingly brazen pirate attacks swelled the level of economic impact and international outcry. Somali piracy's existence has offered an historic challenge to the world. This chapter outlines the conditions that permit piracy, and the historic implications of successful and unsuccessful efforts nations have undertaken against piracy.

Piracy in Antiquity

Maritime piracy—robbery on the high seas—has coexisted with maritime travel and trade as long as seaworthy vessels have plied the oceans.[2] The label of "piracy" is younger than its practice, though—only after experiencing it for a time did early societies recognize a need to criminalize and assign a unique label to high-seas robbery.[3] Hazy boundaries alone separated piracy from legitimate naval warfare as late as the second millennium BC—both were intertwined elements of the struggle for human existence carried out on the sea, and a meaningful world power with the capacity to enforce laws against piracy had not yet emerged.[4]

The concept of piracy as an entity with its own label, distinct from simple maritime trade or warfare, emerged as early as the eighth century BC. As in the modern era, observers who admired the seafaring skill and rich lifestyle of successful pirates sometimes gave them names reflecting more prestige than members of the merchant class.[5] As civilizations stabilized and showed increasing appreciation for the prosperity

---

[2] An expanded definition of piracy comes from the International Chamber of Commerce's (ICC) International Maritime Bureau (IMB): "The act of boarding any vessel with intent to commit theft or any other crime, and with an intent or capacity to use force in furtherance of that act." This definition takes its key elements from the 1982 United Nations Convention on the Law of the Sea (Article 101). See "United Nations Convention on the Law of the Sea," (United Nations Division for Ocean Affairs and the Law of the Sea, 10 December 1982).

[3] The English word "pirate" comes from the Greek πειρατής (peirates), "brigand," derived from πεῖρα (*peira*), "attempt, experience," implying "to find luck on the sea." See Henry George Liddell and Robert Scott, "Peirates," in *A Greek-English Lexicon*, ed. Henry Stuart Jones (Oxford: Clarendon Press, 1940).

[4] Philip De Souza, *Piracy in the Graeco-Roman World* (Cambridge: Cambridge University Press, 2002), 16–17.

[5] As a contemporary example, many observers note that piracy brings a degree of structure and stability to an otherwise dysfunctional Somali society. See Robert Wright, "Piracy Brings Rich Booty to Somalia,"

that comes from trade, the tendency to elevate pirates over merchants subsided, and society allotted greater approbation to preventing the forced seizure of property on the high seas. Concurrently, the leading civilizations created laws that differentiated acceptable plunder (usually of national enemies) from criminal acts of piracy (plunder practiced against allies or one's own people). The laws, to the degree a civilization could enforce them, applied both to pirates originating inside an organized state structure and those not subject to any central government. The latter category in general elicited more admiration, at least in surviving lore. Irrespective of pirates' social esteem, though, Angus Konstam accurately reports, "As in any period, piracy in the ancient world flourished when there was a lack of central control."[6]

Evidence of this historical generalization about piracy exists in its documented presence in areas beyond the reach of major world powers. The first pirate group in recorded history is the Lukkans, sea raiders who operated from the shore of southeastern Asia Minor (modern Turkey). Egyptian scribes recorded their raid of Cyprus in the fourteenth century BC. The Lukkan bases of operations were at the shared frontier of the Egyptians, Assyrians, and Mycenaen Greeks.[7] The Lukkans and their "Sea People" progeny receive credit in some texts for the downfall of several Bronze Age cultures, including destruction of the Mycenaean Greeks and the Hittite Empire.[8] The Sea People did not crush every empire they crossed, though. Konstam credits the decisive battle Egypt's Ramses III fought against these ancient pirates with ending their dominance of the entire Mediterranean and for their subsequent decline after 1186 BC.[9] Success against piracy is doubtless one of the reasons many historians record Ramses III as the greatest of the later Egyptian Pharaohs—he was the first leader to impose enduring order in an anarchic area harboring piracy.

The next civilization defined in part by its response to piracy was ancient Greece. Thucydides, the first historian to adopt a realist's perspective, places a discussion of piracy, naval power, and hegemony in the background discussion for his narrative of the

---

Financial Times (2009), http://www.ftd.de/karriere_management/business_english/:Business-English-Piracy-brings-rich-booty-to-Somalia/494472.html (accessed 2 April 2009).
[6] See Angus Konstam, *Piracy: The Complete History* (Oxford: Osprey Publishing, 2008), 10.
[7] Konstam, *Piracy*, 10.
[8] George Fletcher Bass, *A History of Seafaring: Based on Underwater Archaeology* (London: Thames and Hudson, 1972), 20.
[9] Konstam, *Piracy*, 12.

Peloponnesian War.[10] He places the "first sea fight in history [*sic*]" as happening in the eighth century BC between Corinth and Corcyra. Corinth, long a "commercial emporium" because of its position on the highway for overland travel, exhibited the ability "procure her navy and put down piracy" when sea trade became common, which reflected Corinth's rising influence and ability to exert central control.[11] Athens developed a greater means to combat piracy than did Corinth, reflecting its dominant city-state power, naval superiority, and influence within the Hellas. Thus, Athens could quell the widespread piracy practiced by the Cretans, which plagued all of the eastern Mediterranean.[12] Thucydides' history of the Peloponnesian War is the story of two superpowers—Athens and Sparta—striving for influence and control of the ancient world. As the leading naval hegemon, Athens controlled piracy around the Aegean basin as an extension of its military power and enforcement of regional laws.

Athens' decline saw piracy rise again in the Mediterranean. Decades later, ancient Rhodes, under the protection of Alexander's empire, gave the world the first codified law of the sea.[13] It is a truism to say that the modern formulation of anti-piracy international law remains as much dependent on international agreement enforced through national action as it did in its first inception. What nations perhaps only tacitly note is that any contemporary interpretation of the law of the sea—and all international law—will have origins in the dominant hegemon or superpower that most recently shaped that law.

World leaders continued to mobilize military force and formulate laws against piracy throughout the classical era. In the Roman Republic, a piracy crisis was the impetus that caused the assembly to grant military leaders unprecedented powers. Plutarch recorded the "unrestricted and unlimited power" granted to Pompey to enable him to fight pirates whose "power spread over almost all our sea."[14] Cicero's version of Pompey's campaign against piracy suggests that the undertaking lent credibility to Roman leadership. Both Cicero and Plutarch credit Pompey with eradicating the practice from

---

[10] Thucydides, *The Landmark Thucydides: A Comprehensive Guide to the Peloponnesian War*, ed. Robert B. Strassler, trans. Richard Crawley, 1st Touchstone ed. (New York, NY: Simon & Schuster, 1998), (1.4–1.8).

[11] Thucydides, *The Peloponnesian War*, (1.13.5).

[12] Konstam, *Piracy*, 13.

[13] Jack A. Gottschalk and Brian P. Flanagan, *Jolly Roger with an Uzi: The Rise and Threat of Modern Piracy* (Annapolis, MD: Naval Institute Press, 2000).

[14] Plutarch, *Roman Lives*, trans. Robin Waterfield (Oxford: Oxford University Press, 1999), 244–45.

the Mediterranean in a 67 BC campaign. Cicero's readers learn that Pompey's "undiminished glory" derived from two actions: establishment of another fleet in 62 BC to combat piracy and political-military control of cities to prevent their use as pirate bases.[15] It also galvanized Rome for external military action. After a period of isolationism following the first century BC Roman civil war, Rome projected power outward against a common enemy on her sea.

Along with the remarkable extension of military authority came a notable legal development. Pompey's battle classified pirates with a label still used in contemporary arguments. Cicero records that the late Roman republic's *Lex Gabinia* (Gabinius' Law) called pirates *hostis humani generis*—enemies of the human race—capturing the distaste the general population held for them, and marking the first assertion of "universal jurisdiction."[16] According to Plutarch, Gabinius, who was a close friend of Pompey, gave Pompey "what was not so much a mere naval command, more a full-blown autocracy, involving unregulated absolute power."[17] Pompey's authority reached across land and sea. The same tendency to extend, with a strong legal backing, anti-piracy military power well beyond shore holds true in the present. The six UN Somali piracy resolutions adopted to date give world powers unfettered access to sea and land in the fight against piracy; this reach seems remarkable in the context of modern international law, but recalls the same unbounded authority that Gabinius advocated for Pompey.[18]

Another well-known Roman leader oversaw military and legal efforts against pirates. A young Julius Caesar's involuntary hiatus with Cilician pirates holding him for ransom likely contributed to the urgency with which the Roman triumvirate later pursued

---

[15] De Souza, *Piracy in the Graeco-Roman World*, 179–80. See also Susanna Morton Braund, "Praise and Protreptic in Early Imperial Panegyric: Cicero, Seneca, Pliny," in *The Propaganda of Power: The Role of Panegyric in Late Antiquity*, ed. Mary Whitby (Leiden: Brill, 1998), 74. Even with the liberal license he held as someone who battled and captured hated pirates, Pompey did not destroy all of the pirates he swept from the Mediterranean, but found a way to incorporate them back into a legitimate economy. Through pardons other gentle measures, Pompey persuaded them to surrender and resettled many pirates in Soli, later called Pompeiopolis, now part of southern Turkey.

[16] Douglas R. Burgess, Jr., "Piracy Is Terrorism," *The New York Times*, 5 December 2008, A39. "Universal jurisdiction" is the legal concept that certain crimes are such a threat to all of society that any individual observing the crime must take what immediate action is possible to stop the crime.

[17] Plutarch, *Roman Lives*, 244.

[18] The six resolutions are 1814, 1816, 1838, 1844, 1846, and 1851, all passed in 2008. See "UNSC Resolution 1851," ed. United Nations Security Council (16 December 2008).

pirates.[19] The continued need for a dedicated Roman fleet to combat piracy shows the misplaced optimism of Cicero's claims about Pompey's success, and serves as reminder that the next pirate is never further away than a sea captain's change of attitude. Regardless, the credibility of the Roman republic had a foundation in an artifact of national power: an assertive naval force capable of enforcing anti-piracy laws around the Mediterranean. Such a force remains a defining characteristic of modern world powers.[20] Rome's power and influence derived from its ability to protect its citizens and inhabitants throughout its sphere of influence, and the ability to prevent piracy was an important component of the total effort. To Rome, the Mediterranean was *Mare Nostrum* ("Our Sea"); defense of the sea lines of communication was inextricable from defense of the greater state.

The Middle Ages

Rome's fall signaled the end of its superpower status, ushered in an utter lack of effective centralized control in Europe, and allowed a resurgence of piracy in the Western world. European anarchy in the Early Middle Ages enabled widespread practice by raiders of many nationalities, who enjoyed impunity from legal constraints or any meaningful military resistance.[21] The Vikings, warriors and looters from Scandinavia, ranged all over Europe starting in 793, and eventually attacked as far south as Seville. Only by agreeing to mafia-style protection rackets could the inhabitants of the northern British Isles escape routine Viking raids.[22] Again, piracy thrived under conditions of anarchy, no meaningful military opposition, and a lack of enforceable international law.

Similar conditions prevailed on the southern border of the former empire. Starting about the mid-tenth century, Muslim pirates looted the Mediterranean from the

---

[19] Caesar joked with his captors that he was worth more than the 20 talents of gold they asked for him, inspiring them to raise the ransom to 50 talents (which was paid). His good nature evaporated after he was freed, and he pursued and crucified the pirates. See Plutarch, *Plutarch's Lives of Coriolanus, Caesar, Brutus, and Antonius*, trans. Thomas North and R.H. Carr (Oxford: Clarendon Press, 1906), 45–46.

[20] Alfred Thayer Mahan, *The Influence of Sea Power Upon History, 1660–1783* (Boston: Little, Brown, and Company, 1918), v–vi.

[21] This thesis borrows a common historiographer's definition of the Middle Ages: that period of time from the fall of Rome in the 5th century AD until the beginning of the Early Modern Period in the 16th century. The Middle Ages further divide into three eras: Early (500–1000), High (1000–1300), and Late (1300–1500). See Morris Bishop, *The Middle Ages*, Illustrated ed. (Boston, MA: Houghton Mifflin Harcourt, 2001), 21–22, 42, 114.

[22] Konstam, *Piracy*, 24.

north coast of Africa and established safe havens in modern France, Italy, and Turkey.[23] As with all known piracy, the pirates did not seek ideological supremacy or religious converts—they wanted loot. Precursors of the Barbary Pirates, who would later provide a foil defining decades of US military involvement in world affairs, emerged in the Late Middle Ages. A determined effort by a Genoese naval force to crush Moorish pirates occurred in 1390. Subsequently, a long siege diminished but did not eliminate piracy. Following the Moorish ejection from the Iberian Peninsula in 1492, the former fighting class that had occupied southern Spain lacked an occupation that could provide economic prosperity. Piracy beckoned to fill the need, and the first large-scale pirate raid of Europe by Moors occurred in 1504.[24]

On the opposite side of the globe, the same themes of weak central government, anarchy, and an absence of military power projection enabled another piracy epidemic. The first recorded instance of piracy in the South China Sea dates to AD 589, but it probably existed well before that time, as isolated warlords beyond any dynasty's control had long inhabited the Chinese coast.[25] This earliest record of piracy comes from the Sui Dynasty, when the emperor Wen exercised enough central authority to enforce laws against warlord-sponsored pirates. Wen's control did not last long, and it was not until the Ming Dynasty in the thirteenth and fourteenth centuries that effective imperial control extended to coastal cities and limited piracy near China for appreciable lengths of time. Even when effective domestic central control existed in China, it merely served to push the range of its homegrown pirates further to the west.[26] Chinese pirates initiated over 300 years of attacks in the thirteenth century, sometimes ranging as far west as the African coast of the Indian Ocean. Chinese dynasties with little or no effective legitimate naval power, combined with legions of experienced junk sailors, made China a haven for piracy.

Many other pirate fleets sailed during this era. Goths, Slavs, Ukrainians, Indians, Polynesians—even the Haida and Tlingit tribes of southern Alaska and British Columbia,

---

[23] Ilya V. Gaĭduk, *The Great Confrontation: Europe and Islam through the Centuries* (Chicago: Ivan R. Dee, 2003), 76–78.

[24] Gosse, *The History of Piracy*, 11–12.

[25] Konstam, *Piracy*, 288.

[26] Chinese control of piracy resorted to paying local warlords to stop piracy. In practice, this meant that warlords would stop attacks near China, but would send their fleets further west in search of shipping to attack.

who conducted raids all the way to the modern-day California coast—were among the people groups with significant pirate fleets after antiquity.[27] The civilizations discussed, though, show that the same trend observed in the ancient world continued in the Middle Ages. Piracy followed a pattern of growth when central governance was weak and moved to unregulated fringe areas if the civilizations it plagued were able to reestablish the rule of law on the high seas.

Sixteenth, Seventeenth, and Eighteenth Centuries

Romantic portrayal of pirates in contemporary culture has roots in Elizabethan England. This association with a high point in British civilization serves to mask the underlying anarchy that fueled this particularly active era of piracy. The practice of piracy and reliance on privateering grew substantially during the late sixteenth, seventeenth, and early eighteenth centuries. Captain William Kidd ("Billy the Kidd"), Edward Teach (or Thatch—"Blackbeard"), Bartholomew Roberts ("Black Bart"), and Captain Henry Morgan are all icons of this era—an era when pirates saw easy plunder in the great wealth shipped from the New World on slow-moving and easily attacked merchant ships. Notable centers of pirate operations in the Western hemisphere were the Caribbean and North American colonial coast. Pirates were the most physically fit and capable sailors of their day. These pirates benefitted from the riches of trade routes that extended to West Africa, Madagascar, and the Indian Ocean, and crews were likely to be familiar all these areas.[28] The articles of behavior in force on Captain Kidd's ship reflect the rigid structure and discipline under which successful pirates have always operated.[29] This era, extending from 1560 through the 1730s, also led to a popular infatuation for stories about female pirates, including Mary Read and Anne Bonny, who figure prominently in the historical narrative about piracy in spite of societal norms limiting most women's chances to sail.[30]

---

[27] David Osler, "Flag of Inconvenience," *Lloyd's List*, 29 August 2008.

[28] Jan Rogoziński, *Honor among Thieves: Captain Kidd, Henry Every, and the Pirate Democracy in the Indian Ocean* (Mechanicsburg, PA: Stackpole Books, 2000), 40–42.

[29] Robert Carse, *The Age of Piracy: A History* (New York: Rinehart and Company, Inc., 1957), 6–7. Unfortunately for Kidd, his skill at taking booty outshone his ability to lead men in open society, leading to his disastrous final voyage; see Rogoziński, *Honor among Thieves*, 132–34.

[30] Though sexist by modern standards, at the time such freedom for women offers proof of how far outside social norms pirates operated. See Bonnie Edwards, "Maritime Historian Shares Stories of Female Pirates," *Goldsboro (NC) News-Argus* (3 March 2009), http://www.newsargus.com/news/archives/2009/ 03/03/maritime_historian_shares_stories_of_female_pirates/ (accessed 4 March 2009).

The contrast of disciplined pirate crews against the specter of the unbounded thievery and violence in which those crews engaged is a metaphor for the legal confusion surrounding pirates of this era. Simultaneous celebration and revilement of these practicing pirates hint at a conundrum created by their status under international law, as many called "pirates" today were formally privateers.[31] Historical accounts suggest that the difference today between understanding notable maritime heroes of the era as criminals or heroes depends on whose perspective prevails. *Sir* Francis Drake was an English noble who sailed as a privateer for Queen Elizabeth, but his crews were "at best Her Majesty's pirates" to the Spaniards they plundered.[32] William Kidd, like many other "pirates," was a sanctioned privateer sailing on behalf of England, but his attacks on the merchant vessels of countries with whom England was at peace made him guilty of piracy. Since Drake was probably guilty of similar acts, it seems likely that Drake's superior competence, discretion, and profitability to the Queen saved him from the ignominy and violent death that Kidd and many of his contemporary sailing companions experienced. If within their borders contemporary European states reflected the order and discipline associated with a successful sailing outfit, their embrace of privateering reflects the piratical desperation and anarchic exploitation to which these civilizations' leaders resorted without.

With whatever stigma or honor history records their legacy, the governmental expedient of hiring privateers to achieve national goals resulted in staggering commercial shipping losses. For example, the well-known Jean Bart attacked English and Dutch shipping on behalf of the French during the Nine Years' War; England lost approximately 4,000 merchant ships in the conflict. In the following War of Spanish Succession (1701–1713), England lost about 3,250 merchant ships, again mostly to Spanish privateers.[33] During the Spanish War, England's privateers "far outnumbered the Queen's ships."[34]

---

[31] A privateer is a private ship authorized to attack merchant shipping. A governmental authority at war with one or more nations formally sanctions privateer actions against declared enemies. Authorization comes in the form of "letters of marque," the legal documents authorizing privateer action on behalf of a sovereign. The privateer's only authorization is to attack shipping of enemy nations, though privateers often exceeded this authorization. See Gary M. Anderson and Adam Gifford Jr., "Privateering and the Private Production of Naval Power," *Cato Journal* 11, no. 1 (Spring/Summer 1991): 106.

[32] Carse, *The Age of Piracy*, 3.

[33] Anderson and Gifford Jr., "Privateering and the Private Production of Naval Power," 101–02.

[34] Kenneth R. Andrews, *Elizabethan Privateering: English Privateering During the Spanish War, 1585–1603* (Cambridge: Cambridge University Press, 1964), 21.

American privateers used 1,700 ships during the Revolutionary War to capture almost 2,300 enemy ships.[35] Privateers were efficient at disrupting enemy shipping, and the "prize tax" taken on the spoils they captured benefited the sponsoring nations. With the Spanish treasury empty and Britain lacking the fleet that would make it a superpower in later centuries, the two nations competing for hegemony saw privateering as an absolute necessity. Ocean-going freight constituted the largest share of international trade, just as it does today. A nation unable to secure passage for its merchant ships would wither. Piracy and its cousin privateering—and the ability to defend against both—remained important to national security.

Piracy's "Golden Age," as history books name this era, came about because of factors on the high seas that invariably produce piracy: anarchy rampant with no effective military force that could enforce laws. The anarchy on the high seas stemmed from the inability of any single nation to maintain maritime hegemony for a long period. Spain, then Great Britain, vied for regional influence, but the race for colonial dominance and New World discovery kept the balance of power unsettled for centuries. The era wove a rich tapestry of pirate adventure tales because the striving governments found pirate tactics a useful way to transfer risk. Rather than seeking to abate piracy, states made it a tool of international intercourse. Issuing letters of marque to a privateer allowed an individual "pirate" captain to assume military liability for attacking an enemy nation. The privateer may have given less thought to the political liability he or she assumed, but in practice, crowns could and often did deny the licenses they granted privateers.[36] Questions of risk aside, the frequent pirate attacks of the period arose because there was no national power willing or able to stem the tide of violence and robbery.

Nineteenth Century

The fight against piracy as a general struggle against maritime lawlessness continued into later modern times. While not strictly an anti-piracy effort, contributions of Great Britain and the United States to quelling the outlawed transoceanic slave trade in

---

[35] "Privateers," (17 July 2006), http://www.globalsecurity.org/military/agency/navy/privateer.htm (accessed 31 March 2009). Doubtless this is why the US Constitution provides to the Congress the authority to issue letters of marque: privateering was helpful to the young nation in its struggle for independence.

[36] There is an overwhelming sense that raiders of merchant shipping, whether they were licensed privateers or outlaw pirates, knew what fate they could expect if captured by the nations they attacked: death. The understanding preceded any formal codification in law of privateers' legal status.

the nineteenth century were "among mankind's greatest civilizing achievements."[37] The need and willingness to engage pirates at home and abroad fed from the same desire for rule of law on the high seas that drove the costly US and British naval efforts to end the slave trade. It is no coincidence that piracy's decline happened when it did. Although Britain's efforts against piracy and the slave trade were not free of ideological impulse, the power and will to crush both arose from the nation's desire and its ability to achieve superpower status. Free access to open oceans supported legitimate trade; the end of the slave trade meant that international prohibitions on objectionable behavior again carried the force of law. Both trends served Britain's national interests. Britain could project power around the globe, and an artifact of that power projection manifested in becoming the enforcer of international law that eliminated piracy on a significant portion of the world's oceans.

It is likewise without coincidence that an anti-piracy campaign marked the rise of another superpower. The most famous US effort against pirates took place off the Barbary Coast. Max Boot claims that the clandestine boarding and burning of the *Philadelphia*, which had been captured by the Barbary pirates and anchored in the port of Tripoli, "reverberated from one corner of the globe to the other, gaining newfound respect for the nascent American navy."[38] American action against the Barbary pirates started at the beginning of the nineteenth century.[39] The proximate motivation for the action was economic. By 1801, the United States had paid over $2 million—over one fifth of US annual revenue at the time—in ransom to retrieve ships held captive off the North African coast.[40] The first US foray into international military affairs, involving the nascent US Navy and Marine Corps, came when the nation decided its interests lay in global access that would enable free trade. As Boot's historical perspective notes, this response signaled to the world a US commitment to international affairs not yet seen since the young nation's founding. By 1827, enhanced US Navy capabilities allowed

[37] David B. Rivkin, Jr. and Lee A. Casey, "Pirates Exploit Confusion About International Law," *The Wall Street Journal*, 19 November 2008.

[38] Max Boot, *The Savage Wars of Peace: Small Wars and the Rise of American Power* (New York: Basic Books, 2002), 5.

[39] Alex Beam, "It Takes a Pillage," *The Boston Globe* (2009), http://www.boston.com/lifestyle/articles/ 2009/01/13/it_takes_a_pillage/ (accessed 13 January 2009). At the time, a wooden leg and a parrot on the shoulder were not ironically anachronistic.

[40] "Privateers."

elimination of piracy from all domestic coasts and the Caribbean Sea.[41] The determination of Britain, the existing superpower, and the United States, the rising superpower, to enforce a rule of law supporting access to the open ocean for all who took to the sea ended most piracy in the Western Hemisphere. The results of that decision, with a few minor but notable exceptions, endure to the present day.

Western progress in enforcing international law and stopping piracy stands in stark contrast with an Eastern failure to do either. The scourge of piracy in the Far East that began in the Middle Ages continued into the nineteenth century. A 10,000-man pirate coalition existed during the Qing dynasty in 1804. Famine, internal fighting, and opposition by the legitimate Qing navy conspired to marginalize Chinese piracy by 1820, but it never subsided the same way it did in the West. Pirates of the *Orang Laut*, a Malay ethnic group living in Indonesia, practiced piracy that controlled shipping in the Straits of Malacca until the turn of the twentieth century.[42] At the periphery of empire where British influence tapered off, anarchy made the lawlessness of piracy moot to innocent traders. Piracy endured as a common feature of life on the sea, one that has endured as long as Western freedom from the crime.

Twentieth and Early Twenty-First Centuries

US-led efforts against piracy in the twentieth century have roots in a nineteenth century lineage. In addition to the US commitment evident in its fight against the Barbary Pirates, the young country cautiously embraced the principles of international law. The 1856 Declaration of Paris banned privateering, and quickly gained the wide acceptance necessary to make it an integral part of the body of international law. The United States saw privateering rise again under the anarchic conditions of the Civil War: the Confederate States of America defied convention in briefly issuing letters of marque to authorize attacks against Union merchant shipping.[43] The repetitive lesson is that international law means little, absent a government able to enforce it. After this brief resurgence of privateering, American law formally banned prizes for sinking enemy

---

[41] David Marley, *Pirates and Privateers of the Americas* (Santa Barbara, CA: ABC-CLIO, 1994).

[42] Eda Green, "Borneo: The Land of River and Palm," *Project Canterbury* (1909), http://anglicanhistory.org/asia/sarawak/green/01.html (accessed 2 April 2009).

[43] The United States did not sign the Declaration of Paris, and US-proffered amendments went unheeded, though by 1898 President McKinley announced that the United States would abide by the terms of the agreement during the Spanish-American War. William Morrison Robinson, Jr., *The Confederate Privateers* (New Haven, CT: Yale University Press, 1928), 327–29.

merchant ships in 1899.[44] Modern naval capabilities, including the submarine, undercut the economics of privateering worldwide throughout the twentieth century, and the preferred method for sinking merchant ships during WWI and WWII was *guerre de course* carried out by states' warships and submarines.[45] World governments have been out of the business of attacking merchant shipping as a way to hurt enemies since the world wars; such attacks since the mid-twentieth century have been piracies, not privateering.

The large wars of the twentieth century had the effect of limiting piracy by imposing order on a grand scale. In the massive military mobilization of WWII, the thousands of ships plying the oceans in a military effort to restore international order had a second-order effect of deterring pirates. In the Cold War, the side effects of superpower interest in a bipolar world continued to make shipping channels secure. In this case, the edges of "empires" were unsuitable for piracy: nowhere did the superpowers pay closer attention to each other and enforce order than at their shared periphery. The end of the Cold War saw decreased tensions on the world's shared maritime highways, but also ushered in an era of decreased superpower attention there. Thus, it is not surprising that conditions of anarchy caused by insufficient hegemonic interest arose after the Cold War, and that piracy again became a problem of worldwide interest in the last decade of the twentieth century.

The first alarms over piracy in the late twentieth and early current century rang not in Somalia but in the Far East, in response to a trend observed at the end of the 1990s. Statistics from the 2000 Annual Report of the IMB revealed 469 piracy incidents, a 56 percent increase over 1999 and four times the number reported in 1991.[46] The coastal waters around Indonesia and the Straits of Malacca (between Malaysia and the Indonesian island of Sumatra), were the bodies of water most prone to pirate attack. In 2000, 220 attacks occurred in the Straits of Malacca, which carries one third of global shipping and half of the world's oil, and 150 occurred there in 2003.

---

[44] "Privateers."

[45] *Guerre de course* (literally, "War of race") in this thesis describes commerce raiding by a flagged navy. In the twentieth century, responsibility for commerce raiding during war shifted from a coalition of warships and privateers to the exclusive domain of nations' flagged navies.

[46] Robert C. Beckman, "Combatting Piracy and Armed Robbery against Ships in Southeast Asia: The Way Forward," *Ocean Development and International Law* 33 (2002): 317.

When the incident rate again increased in the first half of 2004, Indonesia, Malaysia, and Singapore organized an unprecedented cooperative effort to combat piracy with a multinational force. This force, called Operation Malsindo, was the first notable instance of a cooperative regional venture against piracy in the Far East. The operation included a commitment from the three signatory countries to maintain five to seven ships year-round in the Straits of Malacca. Cooperation among the various countries' militaries came by creating a hotline, which has proven particularly effective when one navy is in pursuit of a pirate ship headed toward another part of the anti-piracy force. The three nations encouraged further international cooperation, though Malaysia and Indonesia immediately rejected Singapore's suggestion that the United States participate in the effort.[47]

These efforts paid immediate dividends. Attacks near Indonesia dropped to 79 in 2005 and 50 in 2006.[48] The IMB noted with satisfaction that piracy fell in 2005 to its lowest level in six years, "despite a rise in some areas."[49] IMB director Pottengal Mukundan, by many accounts today's most stalwart spokesman against piracy, attributed the drop in attacks—which fell to only 12 in the Straits of Malacca—to a "more proactive" approach taken by many countries concerned with piracy.[50] In 2007, the positive tone continued, with the IMB report noting a "steady decrease" of reported incidents for all of Southeast Asia, including the Straits of Malacca.[51] Captain Mukundan continued his praise in the 2008 report: "Indonesia should be applauded for its sustained efforts in curbing piracy and armed robbery in its waters."[52]

This is fair praise, but the progress is unsurprising. The economic prosperity of this region enabled the nations around the Straits of Malacca to make a stand against

[47] "Indonesia, Malaysia, Singapore Launch Coordinated Patrol of Malacca Strait," *The Jakarta Post* (2004), http://yaleglobal.yale.edu/display.article?id=4271 (accessed 11 February 2009).
[48] International Maritime Board, "Piracy Map 2005," (London: International Chamber of Commerce, 2005). See also the 2006 map.
[49] "2005 Annual Report on Piracy and Armed Robbery against Ships," (Kuala Lumpur: International Maritime Bureau, 31 January 2006).
[50] "Iraq Declared New Piracy Hotspot," *International Chamber of Commerce* (2006), http://www.iccwbo.org/iccfgbd/index.html (accessed 3 April 2009).
[51] "2007 Annual Report on Piracy and Armed Robbery against Ships," (Kuala Lumpur: International Maritime Board, 31 January 2008). Malaysia was a bit more optimistic, claiming that there were no pirate attacks in the Straits of Malacca; see Marcus Hand, "Eyes in the Sky See Strait Attacks Slashed to Zero," *Lloyd's List*, 15 April 2008.
[52] "2008 Annual Report on Piracy and Armed Robbery against Ships," (Kuala Lumpur: International Maritime Bureau, 31 January 2009).

anarchic conditions that permit piracy. Indonesia, Malaysia, and Singapore are unlikely to highlight the fact in press releases, but the growing regional hegemony of China and its visible naval presence in and around the South China Sea also serve the same ends. Military might in combination with rule of law strangles piracy.

However, this thesis is concerned with those areas responsible for keeping the worldwide piracy rate high in spite of the Far East success story. A closer look at African piracy provides useful perspective for this investigation. The IMB's 2004 report noted that there were 28 pirate attacks reported in Nigerian waters, a decrease from 39 in 2003. In spite of the decrease, the report characterized Nigeria as "the most dangerous area in Africa for piracy and armed robbery at sea."[53] Those observations changed the next year. In its 2005 annual report, the IMB noted that 35 reported attacks in Somalia made it the second most dangerous place in the world for piracy, claiming Nigeria's dubious distinction as the most dangerous area in Africa. In what seemed like a drastic and effective recommendation at the time, the report went further to recommend that commercial ships "stay at least 200 nautical miles offshore" to avoid attacks by Somali pirates.[54]

Conclusion

The brief summary of piracy sketched above offers evidence of its characteristics germane to this analysis. Piracy's incessant recurrence around the globe in several periods of history demonstrates its enduring nature. The ebb and flow in number and severity that pirate attacks have exhibited, rising in one area and falling in another, show that piracy is cyclic. The notable efforts of world powers to become involved in fighting piracy teach of its significance as a national security concern. From Pompey's reign until the US response to the Barbary Coast pirates, nations and leaders who would exercise hegemony in an area communicated the desire and demonstrated the ability to perform the anti-piracy role with a convincing response near to or far from their shores. The struggle against piracy is the struggle against anarchy and a fight to uphold international norms. Nations or empires able to lead the fight successfully became hegemons; lately

---

[53] "2004 Annual Report on Piracy and Armed Robbery against Ships," (Kuala Lumpur: International Maritime Bureau, 31 January 2005).
[54] "2005 IMB Annual Report."

they have become superpowers. The rise of piracy in an area where it had been under control portends the decline of a regional power.

The next chapter describes an area of the world where piracy is on the rise. Piracy near Somalia offers a unique challenge for aspiring hegemons or superpowers willing to meet it. It portends the loss of influence for existing hegemons or superpowers unable to rise to the same challenge. This is the historic nature of piracy.

Chapter 2

Somali Piracy

It is remarkable in this first decade of the twenty-first century that we should be having a hearing on the issue of piracy, particularly involving pirate attacks off the coast of Africa. We could almost look back in time 200 years to the first decade of the nineteenth century and ask our predecessors for their advice. Today, we hear from representatives of the Obama administration, while in their day, pirate attacks off Africa were a problem for the new Thomas Jefferson Administration. Both now and then, our resolve is being tested.

—US Senator Jim Inhofe, 5 May 2009

Introduction

This chapter extends the previous chapter's history by discussing the pirates plaguing Somalia in the first decade of the twenty-first century. As chapter 1 anticipates, the rise of piracy originating in Somalia accompanies anarchy and a regional inability to enforce international law. The purpose of this chapter is to demonstrate the extreme nature of Somali piracy and to emphasize how quickly the problem grew to these proportions. It also seeks to differentiate Somali piracy from contemporary piracy in other parts of the world, arguing that it constitutes a unique example of lawlessness worthy of response from a superpower or regional hegemon. Four pertinent areas of analysis provide a picture of Somali piracy: (1) numeric, geographic, and economic scope, (2) criminal patterns, (3) questions of international law, and (4) international commitment. Each area is important in understanding the nature of the US military response to piracy.

Scope

Contemporary piracy off the coast of Somalia is problematic by several measures. In terms of the quantity of attacks, the geographic area affected, the number of nations affected, and the economic impact of piracy, the case of Somali piracy has reshaped world trends. Figure 1 lists International Maritime Bureau (IMB) data for pirate attack reports from 1995 through 2008. The tallest bar on the graph, shown for each year, is the total number of piracy attacks reported to the IMB's Piracy Reporting Center (PRC) and compiled in the IMB's annual piracy reports.[1] After 2001, data for pirate attacks near Nigeria, Somalia, the Gulf of Aden, and Red Sea appear alongside the overall tallies.[2] The figure reveals at a glance an alarming trend borne out in the shipping press. Attacks in areas considered piracy hotbeds (Indonesia and the Straits of Malacca, for example) have diminished in recent years, promising to reduce the overall occurrence of piracy. In spite of the progress in the East, an explosion in attacks since 2005 in the Gulf of Aden and Somali coastal waters kept overall piracy totals climbing. Somali piracy experienced double-digit growth rates every year since 2005.[3] The figure also represents a secondary story: while Nigeria had retained the title of "Most Dangerous Area for African Shipping" through 2005, the waters infested by Somali pirates claimed the title since 2006.

---

[1] There are two consistent sources of piracy data. In addition to the International Chamber of Commerce's IMB, the United Nation's International Maritime Organization (IMO) collects piracy report data worldwide. Numerous political considerations—many centered on Souteast Asian piracy—affect the data, and there are reasons to prefer either set to its rival. For overall trends and reports about Somali piracy, though, both data sets are comparable; the chart uses IMB figures alone for simplicity. For further discussion, see M. Bruyneel, "Current Reports on Piracy by the IMO and the IMB—a Comparison," (Amsterdam: Center for Maritime Research (MARE) and International Institute for Asian Studies (IIAS), 4 September 2003).
[2] Because of the increasing range of Somali pirates and the lack of attacks in the Red Sea, this thesis views Red Sea/Gulf of Aden attacks as occurring in the same domain as Somali attacks. The discussion of geographic scope later in this chapter offers further justification of this view.
[3] Rivkin and Casey, "Pirates Exploit Confusion About International Law," A21.

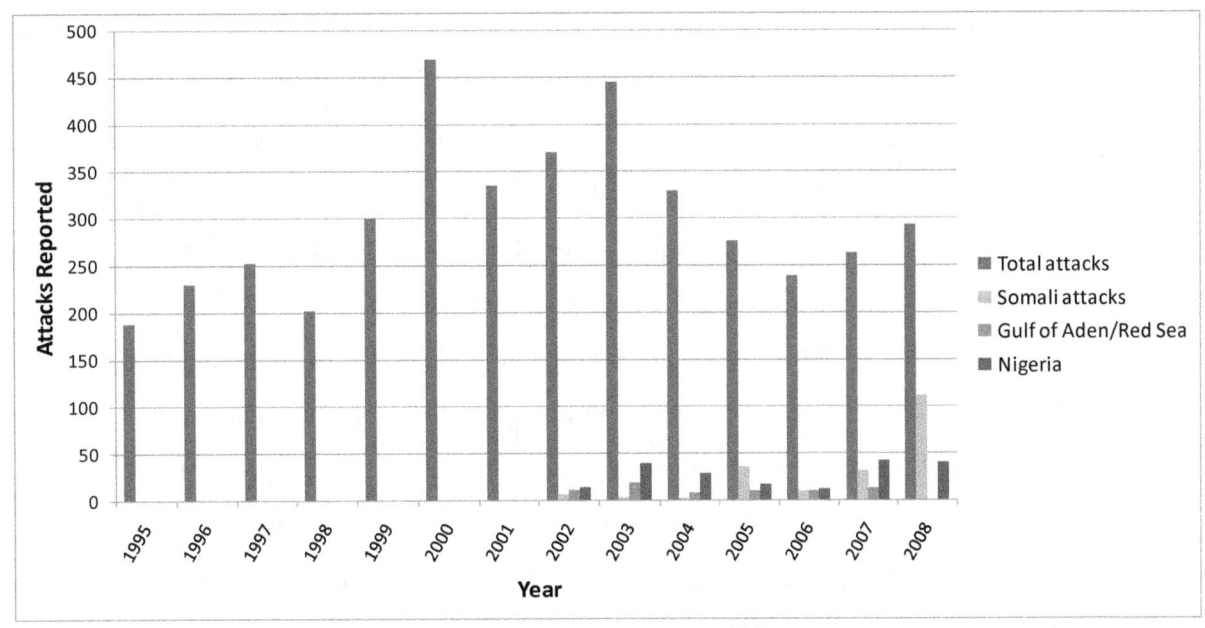

Figure 1: Selected piracy data, 1995–2008

Source: IMB Annual Reports on Piracy and Armed Robbery Against Ships, 1995–2008. *(Note: In 2008 only, the chart groups attacks attributed to Somalia and the Gulf of Aden/Red Sea area as a single area and reports them for Somalia alone. IMB data for 2008 reflect 111 attacks in the combined area.)*

Piracy near Somalia shows no signs of abating in 2009, though dozens of warships from around the world are in place to combat it.[4] Attacks on ships in the first quarter of 2009 were down by some optimistic accounts, but it was poor sailing weather, not military deterrence, that caused the slump.[5] As the weather improved, Somali pirates embarked on an ambitious year of pirate attacks in 2009. Largely due to Somali piracy, worldwide pirate attacks for the first quarter of 2009 more than doubled the 2008 total for

---

[4] Ironically, ships sailing into Somali ports are relatively safe from piracy. Local politics dictate that the officials with the power to fund and allow piracy in a given local area are also the ones who benefit when cargoes arrive unmolested to their local ports. It is also politically untenable to "host" kidnapped crews in the same ports to which they were originally intended to land. Thus piracy of vessels inbound to Somalia is rare in cities like Bossaso (in Puntland), though significant commercial shipments there are also sparse compared to the level of trade plying the seas near coastal Somali cities; see "Somalia: Inside a Pirate Network," *Integrated Regional Information Networks* (2009), http://www.irinnews.org/Report.aspx?ReportId=82339 (accessed 13 January 2009). After the *Maersk Alabama* incident, pirates have been pointedly allowing safe passage for Somalia-bound ships. See Abdi Guled and Andrew Cawthorne, "Somali Pirates Say [They] Freed UAE-Owned Cargo Ship," *The Washington Post* (6 May 2009), http://www.washingtonpost.com/wp-dyn/content/article/2009/05/06/AR2009050600976.html (accessed 7 May 2009).
[5] David Osler, "Fall-Off in Pirate Attacks 'Is Due to Bad Weather'," *Lloyd's List* (2009), http://www.lloydslist.com/ll/news/fall-off-in-pirate-attacks-is-due-to-bad-weather/1235130291373.htm (accessed 3 April 2009).

the same period.[6] During a span of only 48 hours from 1–2 April 2009, pirates seized five ships in wide-ranging attacks around the Gulf of Aden and Indian Ocean.[7] On 6 April, the 32,000-metric ton, British-owned cargo ship *Malaspina Castle* joined the growing ranks of large vessels seized, and its mixed nationality crew of 24 sailors in turn joined over 250 other hostages held along Somalia's modern-day Barbary Coast.[8] The next day, pirates hijacked the *Maersk Alabama*, including twenty US nationals onboard as crew, as the 17,000-ton container ship carried aid to Kenya.[9] The crew retook control of the ship within hours, though Captain Richard Phillips remained a hostage, as four pirates held him captive in the *Alabama's* lifeboat.[10] On 12 April, three US Navy snipers killed the three pirates who remained with Phillips in a dramatic rescue.[11]

Phillips' ordeal put a human face on a problem that had demanded attention in the US media for several months. Although it was by no means the first popular news reporting about Somali piracy, stories about the *Alabama's* crew and Phillips' bravery made a wider audience aware of the scope of Somali piracy, which has grown staggering. The hunting grounds are vast: about 2 million square miles, an area about four times the size of Texas or twice the size of the Caribbean Sea.[12] In figure 2, the dark gray shading shows a locus of points approximately 500 nautical miles from the Somali coast in the Gulf of Aden, Arabian Sea, and Indian Ocean. This gives an appreciation of the size of the pirates' domain, though successful attacks do occur beyond this arbitrary limit. The waters around Indonesia and in the Straits of Malacca, in contrast, constitute a very small region, and comparison suggests in part why anti-piracy task forces from the world's most advanced navies have not been effective in stopping the practice near Somalia.

---

[6] "World Piracy Doubles in First Quarter 2009 Due to Somalia," *Reuters* (21 April 2009), http://uk.reuters.com/article/usTopNews/idUKLL13694920090421 (accessed 8 May 2009).

[7] "Somali Pirates on Hijacking Spree," *Agence France-Presse* (3 April 2009), http://www.google.com/hostednews/afp/article/ALeqM5i_VnXVh5B4FqQzfBeQX-UuQC-tkw (accessed 7 April 2009).

[8] "Pirates Seize British Cargo Ship in Gulf of Aden," *CNN.com* (6 April 2009), http://www.cnn.com/2009/WORLD/africa/04/06/britain.cargo.ship.seized.somalia/ (accessed 7 April 2009).

[9] "Somali Pirates Seize Cargo Ship, 20 US Sailors," *MSNBC.com* (2009), http://www.msnbc.msn.com/id/30103371/ (accessed 8 April 2009).

[10] Siobhan Gorman and Sarah Childress, "American Captain Tries to Escape from Sea Pirates," *The Wall Street Journal*, 11 April 2009, A5.

[11] Liz Halloran, "Obama Wins First Pirate Battle. More to Come," *National Public Radio* (13 April 2009), http://www.npr.org/templates/story/story.php?storyId=103055832 (accessed 14 April 2009).

[12] Mohamed Omar Hajii, "The Ultimate Solution of Piracy and Extremism," *Somaliland Press* (2009), http://somalilandpress.com/1172/the-ultimate-solution-of-piracy-and-extremism (accessed 22 January 2009).

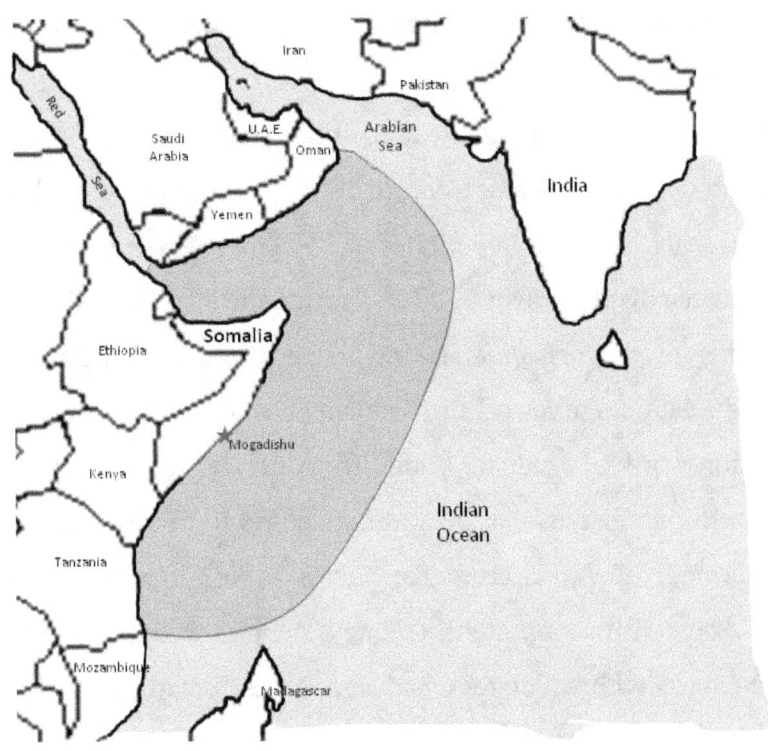

Figure 2: Range of Somali pirates
Source: Author's original work

The next remarkable facet of Somali piracy is the kinds of ships attacked. John Burnett penned much of *Dangerous Waters*, a 2002 description of contemporary piracy, onboard the British-owned *Montrose*, a ship known as a very large crude carrier (VLCC). These carriers, which transport 60 percent of the world's oil, measure over 300 yards long, displace 300,000 tons, and carry over 2 million barrels of oil on a single journey.[13] When he wrote the book, Burnett considered the devastating economic and environmental consequences possible if inexperienced pirates seized and crashed a VLCC in the narrow Straits of Malacca. In spite of this nervous speculation, the book's prevailing tone is that VLCCs are unlikely targets of piracy—their captains and crews possess a "sense of invincibility."[14] With the *Montrose* an improbable target for pirates, it becomes a mere backdrop for a book dealing with attacks against smaller vessels.

---

[13] Although they are enormous, VLCCs are not the world's largest ships. That distinction goes to another tanker: the ultra-large crude carrier (ULCC), which displaces 320,000–550,000 tons. See Joe Evangelista, "Scaling the Tanker Market," *Surveyor* 4, no. 1 (Winter 2002): 5.
[14] John S. Burnett, *Dangerous Waters: Modern Piracy and Terror on the High Seas* (New York: Penguin Putnam, Inc., 2002), 12.

These attacks follow a pattern common to piracy at the turn of the century: the boarding lasts for minutes or hours, and the pirates' take consists of cash or valuables, usually amounting to around $5,000.[15]

Burnett's book might have contained increased personal drama if he had waited a few years to complete his research. In 2008, the aura of invincibility enjoyed by VLCCs evaporated with the seizure by pirates of MV *Sirius Star*, a 318,000-ton crude tanker. Three times the displacement of a US aircraft carrier and possessing a freeboard over 10 meters in height, the *Sirius Star* is the largest ship ever hijacked.[16] Somali pirates seized the ship 450 nautical miles off the Kenyan coast on 15 November 2008. It was carrying $110 million worth of crude oil bound for America, and pirates initially asked for more than $30 million ransom.[17] The captors released the *Sirius Star* on 9 January 2009, its crew unharmed, after an aircraft dropped $3 million in ransom money on the vessel's deck. After carefully counting the money, the pirates departed in the same kind of motorized skiffs with which they had seized the ship, although some met an ironic fate attempting to make land.[18]

The *Sirius Star* is not the only ship to attract attention for its size or cargo. Another well-known pirate attack near Somalia in 2008 was against MV *Faina*, a Ukrainian freighter with a cargo of antiaircraft guns, rocket-propelled grenades, and 33 Russian T-72 tanks "almost certainly bound for south Sudan (with Kenyan government help)."[19] Pirates seized the ship on 25 September, and their ransom demands started at $20 million, a typical starting value. Atypically, because of the weapons onboard, American and Russian warships docked alongside it near the Somali coast to ensure pirates did not remove any cargo from the ship, but never attempted to board or otherwise

---

[15] Dennis M. LaRochelle, Jack A. Gottschalk, and Brian P. Flanagan, "The Economic Cost," in *Jolly Roger with an Uzi* (Annapolis, MD: Naval Institute Press, 2000), 88.

[16] Andrew England and Robert Wright, "Pirates Seize Another Ship in Gulf of Aden," *Financial Times* (17 November 2008), http://us.ft.com/ftgateway/
superpage.ft?page=2&criteria_name=text&criteria_value=%22gulf+of+aden%22. *Freeboard* is the distance from a ship's waterline to its main deck or weather deck. On a small boat, it is the distance between the water level and the top of the boat's side. See "Freeboard," in *Merriam-Webster's Collegiate Dictionary* (Springfield, MA: Merriam-Webster, Inc., 2003).

[17] "Ahoy There," *The Economist*, 22 November 2008.

[18] "Body of a Somali Pirate, Carrying $153,000 of a Ransom, Washes Ashore," *The New York Times*, 12 January 2009, A7. The fate of the Sirius Star pirate gang is instructive. Five pirates drowned in trying to return to shore in a small boat with their shares. One body recovered had $153,000 in a plastic bag. Three made it to shore but lost their share of the ransom.

[19] "Ahoy There."

interfere in negotiations. Pirate spokesman Sugule Ali on 11 January 2009 declared to the Associated Press that crew members were healthy and ready to be released after negotiations were complete.[20] That promise proved true. On 5 February, following an airdrop of $3.2 million, the pirates calmly counted the money, departed the ship, and left the entire crew unharmed.[21]

Both the *Sirius Star* and *Faina* incidents ended well enough, but Somali piracy heralds an era where no ship is too big to become a prize. The genius of the pirates lies in their conversion of all ships into fungible assets through a ransom mechanism. The *Sirius Star's* crude oil and the *Faina's* military weapons have value on the black market, but demanding air-dropped cash eliminates the need to pump oil off a ship or to fence stolen tanks. The Somali pirates have found a way to extract the most fungible resource of all from the ships they steal: US dollars. They do not even have to melt down gold coins in the way British pirates turned Spanish Galleons into formless gold ingots.

The realization that all ships are potential targets for Somali pirates affects the economics of shipping. Piracy is a macroeconomic phenomenon that touches individuals unevenly. The lives lost to pirate attacks near Indonesia in past years seem tragic to the families experiencing them, even though cold, calculating reports about piracy mention the diminishing effects of piracy in that area. The same analogy applies to the economics of piracy. The ransoms and lost profits associated with a single hijacked ship seem large to outside observers, but pale in comparison to the huge scale of the global shipping industry. The cost of a single loss is therefore small in the eyes of the insurance industry that underwrites the world's shipping. LaRochelle argued in 2000 that nations and shipping companies did not do more to combat piracy simply because it was not cost effective.[22] Increased insurance premiums fit comfortably into the cost of doing business. Negotiation and paying ransoms in good faith decreases the chances of pirates killing kidnapped sailors, and shipping companies, their focus on profit aside, do seem to want to protect their employees, if only to prevent a restive labor market.

---

[20] "Body of a Somali Pirate..." A7.
[21] Christa Case Bryant, "Somali Pirates Free Hijacked Ukrainian Ship," *The Christian Science Monitor* (2009), http://features.csmonitor.com/globalnews/2009/02/05/somali-pirates-free-hijacked-ukrainian-ship/ (accessed 9 February 2009).
[22] LaRochelle, Gottschalk, and Flanagan, "The Economic Cost," 93.

Even with the explosion of piracy near Somalia and multiple millions of dollars in ransoms, the reality that piracy exacts low cost relative to the shipping industry remains true. While insurance premiums on ships going through the Gulf of Aden increased tenfold in 2008, the raise is insignificant to many shippers.[23] One reason is economies of scale. Even with increased insurance rates, it costs only pennies to ship a large container of consumer goods around the world. Another reason is the geography of Africa. Avoiding the shipping corridor through the Gulf of Aden and the shortcut to the West through the Red Sea and Suez Canal adds between five and 10 days to a trip from Asia to Europe, with each extra day at sea costing about $30,000.[24] Redirecting around the Cape of Good Hope can add $1 million to the cost of a journey for a large container ship. Insurance premium increases, which have risen as much as 0.5 percent of a ship's total value, add hundreds of thousands of dollars to premiums, but are still smaller than the cost of taking the alternate route.[25]

This is not to say that the piracy spike has not generated alarm in shipping circles. Industry advocates rarely miss an opportunity to cite the latest statistics in trade magazines, or mention with an ominous air that seven to twelve percent of the world's annual oil supply transits the Gulf of Aden.[26] Conferences declaim that attacks have pushed shipping insurance premiums along the route to "near-prohibitive levels" and have damaged "littoral economies" by forcing vessels around the Cape of Good Hope.[27] Another tangential victim is the fishing industry, which pirates subdued by the capture and subsequent return of a tuna-fishing vessel for a $1 million ransom.[28] Along with these inconveniences come benefits. The first is that the inadvertent fishery conservation

---

[23] Miles Costello, "Somalian Piracy Cripples Shipping with Tenfold Insurance Cost Rises," *The Times*, 11 September 2008, 23.

[24] Mohamed Omar Hajii, "The Ultimate Solution of Piracy and Extremism."

[25] The total value of a large merchant ship (vessel alone) ranges typically from $10 to $100 million. See Shreya Roy Chowdhury, "Piracy Fallout of Illegal Fishing," *The Times of India* (2009), http://timesofindia.indiatimes.com/World/Rest_of_World/_Piracy_fallout_of_illegal_fishing/articleshow/4034251.cms (accessed 28 January 2009).

[26] Brian Wilson and James Kraska, "Anti-Piracy Patrols Presage Rising Naval Powers," *YaleGlobal* (2009), http://yaleglobal.yale.edu/display.article?id=11808 (accessed 11 February 2009).

[27] Michael Heath, "Anti-Piracy Group Meets at UN to Plan Action in Somali Waters," *Bloomberg.com* (2009), http://www.bloomberg.com/apps/news?pid=20601101&sid=aecphtP0uYZk&refer=japan (accessed 16 January 2009).

[28] Many pirates are former tuna anglers who found more economic promise in piracy syndicates.

effect caused by Somali pirates has likely led to a recovery of dwindling tuna stocks.[29] The second is private sector growth potential: the former Blackwater Worldwide and other private security firms have approached shippers and insurance firms about protecting ships in Somali waters.[30] The scope of piracy—most notably the numbers of attacks, the geographic area affected, and the potential economic effects—leads to a discussion about how the Somali piracy differs from other parts of the world.

Somali Pirates' Unique Business Plan

Pirates in Somalia have developed a new scheme for perpetrating their crime. The IMB describes three types of piracy: (1) low-level armed robbery, (2) medium-level armed assault and robbery, and (3) major criminal hijack.[31] The first kind, termed "maritime muggings" by Captain Jayant Abhyankar of the IMB, constituted the vast majority of piracy attacks at the turn of the century and often yields the $5,000 average take mentioned above.[32] The second type involves better-organized pirates, often working from mother ships, and may involve an effort to steal some of a ship's cargo (especially fungible commodities) in addition to stealing navigation equipment and contents of the ship's safe. The third type is the most brazen, requires the most talent, and usually results in a ship's complete loss to its original owners. Somali pirates have eschewed the first type of piracy—it does not pay enough to bother. The second and third types require national shipyards or concealed ports that permit clandestine "reflagging" of a stolen ship. Somalia has neither of these, so pirates have adapted to practice a new form of hijacking.

---

[29] Danilo Masoni, "Munich Re Sees Piracy Pushing up Marine Premiums," *Reuters* (2009), http://uk.reuters.com/article/rbssFinancialServicesAndRealEstateNews/idUKLS75104120090128 (accessed 28 January 2009). The Indian Ocean tuna industry is worth $6 billion annually and provides one quarter of the world's tuna.

[30] August Cole, "Blackwater Plans Effort against Piracy," *The Wall Street Journal*, 3 December 2008, A11. Blackwater has a ship to challenge pirates: the 183-foot McArthur, acquired in 2006, which carries two helicopters and the rigid-hull inflatable boats favored by naval commandoes. Blackwater's database of contractors includes former Navy SEALs and Coast Guard personnel. Recent troubles on the Xe (the company formerly called Blackwater) ship caused the company to shelve anti-piracy plans in mid-2009. See Bill Sizemore. "Sailors on Blackwater Anti-Piracy Ship Claim Harassment." In *The Virginian-Pilot*. (Place Published, 14 May 2009), http://hamptonroads.com/2009/05/sailors-blackwater-antipiracy-ship-claim-harrassment (accessed 20 May 2009).

[31] I.D.H. Wood, "Piracy Is Deadlier Than Ever," *United States Naval Institute Proceedings* 126, no. 1 (January 2000): 60.

[32] LaRochelle, Gottschalk, and Flanagan, "The Economic Cost," 88.

Thus, it is not that ship hijacking *per se* is new, but the ship hijackings associated with Somalia are both qualitatively and quantitatively separate. The IMB reports statistics on ship hijackings going back to 1991. In its 1997 annual report, a then-record 14 hijackings appear.[33] Popular articles on so-called "phantom ships" document a pattern where pirates seize a ship, often killing crewmembers they cannot co-opt, and sell the ship and cargo on the black market or use it as a platform for further piracy attacks.[34] The problem developing off the African coast, however, does not follow this pattern either.

In Somalia, while ship hijacking is almost the only purpose pirates have, Somalis' aims differ from other types of hijackers. The pirates are not intent on selling ships, stealing the cargo, or even attaining a platform for further attacks. Instead, they have established a unique pattern that involves threatening a ship with heavy armament, boarding it, holding its crew captive, and sailing it into Somali territorial waters. With the ship anchored off the coast, the well-organized pirates begin negotiations with ship owners for ransom money. They usually keep crewmembers alive, well fed, and relatively comfortable while they wait for the delivery of ransom. Invariably, the pirates let the ship and crew go without further harm after ransom money arrives. Pirates in other areas of the world do not practice this hold-for-ransom pattern. Because Somali pirates attempted over 100 attacks in 2008 and exacted more than $1 million on average each time they were successful, one might reasonably conclude their tactics have ushered in a new era in the history of piracy. Knowledge of piracy's history reveals that this is a fallacy. Though appearing novel in the current context, the Somali business model is an old one—recall that the Barbary Pirates used the exact same approach on American ships in the eighteenth and nineteenth century. Likewise, the pirates who stoked Julius Caesar's wrath held him for ransom. Just as the "new" Somali piracy business model has deceived journalists, so legal experts have agonized about seemingly new questions of law raised by piracy—previous civilizations have asked and answered these as well.

---

[33] "1997 Annual Report on Piracy and Armed Robbery against Ships," (Kuala Lumpur: International Maritime Bureau, 31 March 1998).

[34] The phantom ship problem most often occurs in an area of the Far East known as the Hong Kong-Luzon-Hainan (HLH) Triangle. See William Langewiesche, "Anarchy at Sea," *The Atlantic*, September 2003, 66.

International Law, Terrorism, and the Disposition of Somali Pirates

Piracy, as mentioned in chapter 1, receives healthy attention in the body of international maritime law. This does not mean that the legal disposition of pirates is always a simple matter, though. Legal concerns have slowed or prevented the US military response to piracy, as well as that of several other nations, and efforts to clarify this confusion occupied several months. After exhibiting an unwillingness to detain pirates at all, on 26 January 2009, the United States brokered a deal with Kenya, who agreed to try any Somali pirates captured by the US Navy. Kenyan prime minister Raila Odinga cited rising insurance premiums and increased risk to ships bound for Mombassa, Kenya's main port, as incentive for the bargain.[35]

An argument often put forward about the legal status of pirates is one that equates them with terrorists and suggests in-kind, extraordinary measures to handle them. Douglas Burgess takes this tack, arguing that the historical legal interpretation of pirates as criminals whose actions affect international society puts them in the same category as terrorists.[36] Burgess advocates for the legal reasoning offered by Judge Nicholas Trott, who presided over a British pirate trial in 1718: "It is lawful for any one that takes them, if they cannot with safety to themselves bring them under some government to be tried, to put them to death."[37]

Burgess is not alone. Many experts have looked for a nexus between Somali piracy and maritime terrorism. *The Economist* opined, "[P]iracy will be bad news even for Somalia, accelerating the Talibanisation of the south by armed Islamist groups as more secular-minded gunmen abandon their poorly paid defense of Mogadishu for adventures at sea."[38] Intelligence analyst John McCreary has expressed frustration with the US policy of seeking a legitimate international partner in bringing pirates to trial, citing the examples of other countries that "just shoot the pirates or blast them with water cannons. They make no pretense about the need to bring pirates to justice. The sea itself

---

[35] Tom Maliti, "US to Hand over Any Suspected Pirates to Kenya," *Associated Press* (2009), http://www.google.com/hostednews/ap/article/ALeqM5gB7YMEDuCwwY9ncDOtPAkEI4-H2wD95V0C9G0 (accessed 26 January 2009).
[36] Burgess, "Piracy Is Terrorism," A39.
[37] Rivkin and Casey, "Pirates Exploit Confusion About International Law."
[38] "Ahoy There."

is the source of their justice."[39] Rivkin and Casey assert, "The task of prosecuting captured pirates [should be] an easier process, both from a legal and public relations perspective."[40] In general, experts' calls for quick, simple prosecution of pirates (while assuming world-wide approval) rest on an argument that draws a direct line between piracy and terrorism. This link is tenuous.

Peter Chalk, a piracy expert at RAND, lists high-profile maritime terrorist incidents in a study of piracy and maritime terrorism. All but one of the incidents he recounts played a direct role in a terrorist act or enabled the shipment of weapons and supplies to a terrorist organization. His account of the exception, Gerakhan Aceh Merdeka's (GAM) hijacking of the MV *Penrider*, a fully laden oil tanker, stressed that the outcome of the incident was a $52,000 ransom to the former Indonesian separatist terror group.[41] The post-9/11, terror-aware security environment in which Chalk wrote influenced his approach—the report was an effort for the Air Force to cooperate better with the Navy. In the funding milieu of that era, proving a risk of terrorism was a likely way to obtain funding. Even this academic effort attempts to find a link to terrorism that piracy simply does not share.

The logic leading to the pessimism that piracy will feed terrorism is easy to follow, as Chalk concedes, but in reality, it has not materialized in Somalia because of a raft of contravening reasons. The first reason is that Somali pirates are already in control of the economy in which they operate. They are unlikely to seek partners with whom they can share their hard-fought ransom monies. Second, there is a natural enmity between the Muslim extremists associated with terrorism in the Horn of Africa and pirates. *Sharia* law forbids kidnapping or theft, and threatens pirates with the death penalty, adding another reason why terrorists and pirates are not likely to collaborate.[42] In reality, a nexus between piracy and terrorism has not emerged—it remains an

---

[39] John McCreary, "NightWatch," (AFCEA Intelligence, 29 January 2009). McCreary's sentiment is common among those who follow piracy matters, but his facts are suspect. For example, he describes gangs of pirates "that range up and down the Red Sea," although few pirate attacks ever occur there. The IMB's electronic map of pirate attacks shows that vessels in the Red Sea remain relatively unmolested, either waiting anxiously to enter the perilous Gulf of Aden or breathing easier for having just cleared it.
[40] Rivkin and Casey, "Pirates Exploit Confusion About International Law."
[41] Peter Chalk, "The Maritime Dimension of International Security: Terrorism, Piracy and Challenges for the United States," in *Project Air Force* (Santa Monica, CA: RAND, 2008), 47–52.
[42] Chalk, discussion with author.

economic, not ideological, crime. If nations insisted on establishing an unambiguous terror motivation for piracy before acting, most piracy in the world would continue unchecked.

Attempts to paint piracy with terrorism's broad brush, therefore, are inaccurate and do not resolve legal questions. As LaRochelle writes, maritime piracy "is, has been, and always will remain, at its heart, a business endeavor."[43] Picking up pirates at sea is not like detaining al Qaeda terrorists, and pirates have made that point to the world with humane ethics toward hostages and a modest public relations effort.[44] The next chapter takes up a discussion of the roots of US restraint regarding piracy, but it is here worth questioning some of the reasons given for this restraint, as they are legal arguments.

The degree of latitude that Somalia and the UN have granted to any nation willing to prosecute pirates is remarkable. A specific resolution authorizes hot pursuit into Somali territorial waters and even onto the land; Somalia's provisional, recognized government has campaigned for and applauded the resolution's passage.[45] With this extraordinary license applied to a specific situation, it is astounding that the United States and many other nations have publically agonized over the legal status of Somali pirates. The legal confusion persisted even as military involvement steadily built, and, until mid-2009, damped US military responses.

This thesis views the so-called confusion as political smoke and mirrors. According to Northwestern University law professor Eugene Kontorovi, "The nations patrolling the Gulf of Aden have chosen not to prosecute pirates because of the anticipated difficulty and expense."[46] Reading the applicable international conventions reveals that these documents clearly define piracy and encourage states to prosecute the act as a crime. It is true that the United States has not ratified the latest major component

---

[43] LaRochelle, Gottschalk, and Flanagan, "The Economic Cost," 85.

[44] Jeffrey Gettleman, "Pirates Tell Their Side: They Want Only Money," *The New York Times*, 1 October 2008.

[45] Part of the reason for legal confusion stems from the nature of standing international law about piracy. Since privateering (an act of war) was the last serious maritime issue world courts examined, international law treats piracy as an act of war. This limits faster, easier criminal prosecution options. See "European Parliament Moves to Redefine Piracy as Criminal Act," *Lloyd's List*, 30 October 2008. The UN resolution mentioned is Security Council resolution 1816; see Paul Tugwell, "Shipping Unites in 'Crisis Call'," *Lloyd's List*, 19 September 2008.

[46] Douglas S. Malan, "Maritime Attorneys Deal with High Seas Piracy," *The Connecticut Law Tribune* (24 April 2009), http://www.law.com/jsp/law/sfb/lawArticleSFB.jsp?id=1202430155573 (accessed 8 May 2009).

of international law to address piracy, the UN Convention on the Law of the Sea of 10 December 1982 (UNCLOS 1982). In spite of this, the nation accepts the entire agreement as customary international law except part XI, which deals with economic activity and does not contain any language about piracy. UNCLOS 1982 replaced four earlier UN treaties, among these the 1958 UN Convention on the High Seas. Both this treaty and UNCLOS 1982 contained the same substantive language about piracy. Specifically, the agreements allow any nation's navy or designated fleet to stop piracy and apprehend pirates. Further, captured pirates are subject to trial in the courts and under the laws of the capturing country.

With this clear language, the approbation of the international community, and encouragement from the legitimate government of Somalia, it is difficult to comprehend what legal difficulty the United States or any other nation finds in prosecuting pirates. Perhaps there is discomfort looking back to the Declaration of Paris, which conflates piracy with an act of war. Perhaps there is a misguided question about the Posse Comitatus Act.[47] Whatever its source, this confusion need not persist. Recall the differentiation between piracy and privateering presented in chapter 1. Also, recall that hegemons and superpowers have the greatest influence on international law.

The truly perplexing legal question is why the United States looked for opposing legal arguments in an effort to justify a lack of anti-piracy efforts, initially balking from stopping blatant piracy, because it claimed an inability to prosecute accused pirates. If a sensible legal definition of piracy and authority to stop it did not exist, this thesis argues that a superpower like the United States should argue for one. Given that the definition did exist and that the international community supported anti-piracy military action, the United States should have been free of legal concern. A clear upshot of the *Maersk Alabama* saga is that it appears to have overcome US reluctance to try pirates in US courts.[48] Thus, the United States has overcome its self-inflicted problem, but the initial legal hand wringing is troubling. It means either that the nation did not feel it retained the ability to lead in matters of international law or that it had spent some effort looking

---

[47] The Posse Comitatus Act (18 U.S.C. § 1385) prohibits the use of federal military forces to enforce civil law within the United States. The prohibition does not speak to military action overseas; conflating military arrest of the "civilian" pirates with law enforcement inside national boundaries might be a spurious source of confusion.

[48] Benjamin Weiser, "Pirate Suspect Charged as Adult in New York," *The New York Times*, 22 April 2009.

for reasons to ignore Somali piracy. Neither explanation reflects credit on a superpower—inconsistency and hesitance with respect to international law both demonstrate reluctance or inability to lead.

International Involvement and Superpower Attention

The next source of concern lies in the strength of the responses other nations have made to Somali piracy. Active pirates attract daily media attention; images of buccaneers have always sold books and newspapers.[49] Contemporary response is not limited to the culture sections of newspapers, however. The international military response to Somali piracy has been extensive. France has at times aggressively pursued pirates, freeing captured vessels and hostages.[50] Working as part of Operation Atalanta, the European Union's (EU) common defense response to piracy near Somalia, France stopped a pirate attack in progress on 27 January 2009 and arrested nine pirates.[51] This action continues a long series of anti-piracy action off the African coast. French forces have made successful commando-style raids in which they board pirated ships at harbor, overpower pirates, and free the ship without harm to the crew.[52]

The Danish navy also has been involved in fighting Somali piracy, but the creation of a multinational naval force threatened to end this participation because Denmark had not agreed to the common defense structures within the EU. The public uncertainty Denmark aired is typical of many nations' responses to the piracy: an outdated international law concern threatens a practical need. Denmark's response has also followed a common pattern. Rather than remove its naval forces from the effort, Denmark has kept its ship *Absalon* in place, and has dealt with its international law questions by pragmatically agreeing to hand pirates over for trial to the Netherlands, which does participate in EU common defense measures. This tack paralleled the initial US approach to its questions about pirate prosecution and subsequent extradition agreement with Kenya. Denmark exercised its policy before the US Navy did, though,

---

[49] Konstam, *Piracy*, 7.
[50] Rivkin and Casey, "Pirates Exploit Confusion About International Law."
[51] "French Navy Foils Somali Pirate Attack."
[52] "French Troops Kill Somali Pirate to Free Hostages," *Birmingham Post*, 17 September 2008.

turning over five suspected pirates to the Netherlands after a warning flare fired by the *Absalon* caused their boat to catch fire and start sinking.[53]

The Dutch navy sent its own frigate with a crew of 170 to the Gulf of Aden in March to protect shipments of food and other humanitarian aid to Somalia. The Netherlands agreed to try captured pirates on behalf of the Danes, who found themselves without a proper legal process to do so in light of the legal questions mentioned in the previous section.[54] Other nations involved in the battle against piracy include Australia, Britain, Canada, Germany, Greece, Italy, Japan, Korea, Kuwait, Malaysia, New Zealand, Pakistan, , Portugal, Singapore, Spain, Sweden, and Turkey. **Even African countries, never traditional naval powers, have made a united response to piracy.**[55]

As interesting as these contributions are, and as broad a coalition as they represent, this thesis emphasizes the involvement of a few more countries not yet listed. These include China, India, Iran, and Russia; China and Russia are of the greatest importance. **China sent two destroyers and a logistics ship to the Indian Ocean and Gulf of Aden in December 2008.**[56] China began patrol operations on 6 Jan 2009, mainly in support of Chinese merchant ships, but with an offer to escort ships of other nationalities if requested. A representative also issued a strong threat of force to any pirates operating in the area.[57] China later expressed its satisfaction with the anti-piracy force and announced a long-term commitment to naval patrols in the area.[58]

---

[53] "Somali Pirates Extradited to Netherlands," *Voice of America* (2009), http://www.voanews.com/english/2009-02-10-voa43.cfm (accessed 11 February 2009).

[54] "Dutch Courts to Try Pirates Now Held in Denmark," *The International Herald Tribune* (2009), http://www.iht.com/articles/ap/2009/01/15/europe/EU-Netherlands-Pirates.php (accessed 16 January 2009).

[55] "African, Middle East States Seek Legal Reforms to Try Pirates," *EasyBourse* (2009), http://www.easybourse.com/bourse-actualite/marches/african-middle-east-states-seek-legal-reforms-to-try-603591 (accessed 26 January 2009). Twenty-two African and Middle East states opened talks in Djibouti in January 2009 to formulate agreements allowing their courts to try pirates captured by foreign navies.

[56] Wilson and Kraska, "Anti-Piracy Patrols Presage Rising Naval Powers." It was a maneuver reminiscent of China's naval hegemony that extended throughout the Indian Ocean for a brief period after the era of the Warring States; see William H. McNeill, *The Pursuit of Power: Technology, Armed Force, and Society since AD 1000* (Chicago: The University of Chicago Press, 1982), 26.

[57] "China Begins Somalia Piracy Patrols," *Aljazeera.net* (2009), http://english.aljazeera.net/news/asia-pacific/2009/01/200917523146179900.html (accessed 7 January 2009).

[58] "China to Renew Somalia Anti-Piracy Mission," *Associated Press* (2009), http://www.google.com/hostednews/ap/article/ALeqM5i0A_UOu6oEtFNUxbNBFFThfSfCwgD96QCSGO0 (accessed 9 March 2009).

India has been even more active. The warship INS *Tabar* blew up a Somali pirate "mothership" on 18 November 2008 in retaliation for seizing the *Sirius Star*.[59] Suspected pirates, traveling in a vessel towing two high-speed boats like pirates use to board other vessels, brandished rocket-propelled grenade launchers, and eventually fired at the Indian ship. The *Tabar* returned fire and sank the Somali vessel and crew.[60] Indian interest reflects geographic proximity to the troubled region and strong domestic political interest. A high percentage of crew members on hijacked ships are Indian nationals.

Russia abruptly became involved in anti-piracy efforts, and its action seemed to surprise Western observers. In addition to supplying a destroyer to keep a watchful eye on the *Faina* during its Somali hiatus, Russia maintains a fleet of ships to deter piracy in the Gulf of Aden. Russia's commitment, carefully timed to follow a UN call for international help with Somali piracy, dates to late October 2008.[61] Russia's action, met with cautious welcome by shipping firms and other governments, ushered in increased involvement by India, China, and even Iran, all US rivals to some degree, and all seekers of hegemony in their respective geographic regions. The effects of these nations making unexpected announcements that they would send their navies to the Indian Ocean and Gulf of Aden to protect global shipping lanes elicited an intriguing response from the United States.

The Evolution of the US Response to Piracy

The US response to piracy near Somalia has exhibited subtlety, and a nuanced, timeline-based appreciation of this response is critical to the concluding argument offered in chapter 4. A nominal anti-piracy force has operated in the waters around Africa for many years. That is to say, the US Navy policy of keeping open sea-lanes includes an explicit challenge to piracy, and there have been groups of naval ships in the waters around Africa that could perform that mission for the past several decades. However, the actual size of the effort, as well as its timing, is worthy of careful scrutiny. The central argument here is that American efforts, previously small by the standards of national

---

[59] "Ahoy There."
[60] Mohamed Omar Hajii, "The Ultimate Solution of Piracy and Extremism."
[61] "Russian Warship on Somali Pirate Mission to Enter Gulf of Aden," *BBC Worldwide Monitoring*, 26 October 2008.

power, saw a dramatic increase following visible, unexpected Russian and Chinese commitments.

From 2000 to 2008, a single US-sponsored maritime task force maintained responsibility for keeping sea lines of communication around Africa open to trade. Combined Task Force 150 (CTF-150) conducts maritime security operations (MSO) around the Horn of Africa, Gulf of Aden, Gulf of Oman, Red Sea, and Indian Ocean.[62] CTF-150 has its base in Djibouti, includes a conspicuous international presence, rotates command frequently, and has had commanders from France, Spain, the Netherlands, Britain, Pakistan, Canada, and Germany.[63] The task force was the only US answer to Somali piracy until August 2008. Given the enormity of the geographic area affected by Somali piracy and the increasing number of attacks, CTF-150's ships and aircraft alone are insufficient to have much impact on the problem as a whole.[64]

The US Navy's background role in CTF-150 complemented efforts by nations whose positions in foreign policy often align with those of the United States. In August 2008, after pirates had taken four ships off the Somali coast in a 48-hour period, the US Naval Forces Central Command established a Maritime Security Patrol Area (MSPA). The MSPA, which encourages merchant ships to condense their operations within a given area so that available defense assets may better protect them, stressed that it was a coalition effort, and that it stood up in response to calls from the IMB.[65] This deference to an international organization signaled that the US Central Command, which effectively established a framework so that other nations could assist in the protection of shipping with all available assets, had a genuine desire to stress coalition participation.

Later in the fall, continuing a theme of international cooperation, NATO secretary general Jaap de Hoop Scheffer announced restructured intelligence, command, control, and information-sharing procedures among NATO countries conducting anti-piracy operations in October 2008.[66] Since this did not commit additional resources, it was mainly a symbolic gesture, similar to NATO's earlier July 2007 announcement of an

---

[62] CTF-150 consists of approximately 15 vessels, of which six or seven are from the US Navy. MSO includes monitoring, inspecting, boarding, and stopping suspect shipping vessels.

[63] US Fifth Fleet Commander, "Combined Task Force 150," *US Naval Forces Central Command* (2009), http://www.cusnc.navy.mil/command/ctf150.html (accessed 8 April 2009).

[64] Anthony J. Linardi, (Commander, US Navy), in discussion with the author, 12 November 2008.

[65] "Naval Forces Establish Somalia Safety Zone," *Lloyd's List*, 26 August 2008.

[66] "NATO Unveils Maritime Security Mission," *Lloyd's List*, 27 October 2008.

international flotilla of ships prepared to make "an historic 12,500 nautical mile circumnavigation around Africa in response to rising piracy attacks and drug trafficking."[67] Though this may generate approval among some newspaper readers, few military efforts could have less of an effect on piracy than sailing around Africa once with a convoy of warships.

The United States encouraged international efforts, offering copious approval to nine European Union nations who agreed to deploy three frigates, three surveillance ships, and a supply ship shortly after the *Faina* became a victim of piracy.[68] This agreement became the EU's Operation Atalanta, which deployed under British command in December 2008.[69] The United States also offered statements of appreciation for planned anti-piracy involvement from South Korea and Japan, and seemed willing to play the role of traffic director for all nations who would deign to support the international fight against piracy near Somalia.

The passive stance against piracy appeared in an overmatched CTF-150, US hopefulness for better NATO cooperation, and optimism for Operation Atalanta mirrored other messages reflecting isolationist facets of US foreign policy. In 2007, the US Navy publicized that it was increasing its use of "soft power."[70] The presidential campaign season brought constant reminders that the United States was fully involved in two wars for which success or even near-term progress often seemed hopeless. The nation's top military officer, chairman of the Joint Chiefs of Staff, Admiral Michael Mullen, made statements decrying US strategic over-commitment and reminded military personnel of their exhaustion. In December 2008, the US Navy claimed that international law effectively tied its hands with regard to piracy. At that time, the US Navy cited lack of suitable Somali authorities, to whom military forces could return pirate suspects for prosecution, as a main reason why it would not engage in direct anti-piracy operations. Chapter 4 will offer evidence that national leaders likewise shared sentiments of current

---

[67] Brian Reyes, "NATO Warships Respond to Piracy Threats Off Africa," *Lloyd's List*, 23 July 2007.
[68] Jamie Smyth, "EU Agrees on Mission to Combat Piracy," *The Irish Times*, 3 October 2008.
[69] Richard Norton-Taylor, "Britain to Lead Fleet of EU Warships to Tackle Pirates," *The Guardian* (2008), http://www.guardian.co.uk/world/2008/nov/19/piracy-somalia-eu-operation-atalanta (accessed 8 April 2009).
[70] Gordon Lubold, "US Navy Aims to Flex 'Soft Power'," *Christian Science Monitor*, 27 December 2007.

and rising international affairs elites, favoring an isolationist US stance as part of a strategy designed to increase international support for US policies.

The tenor of US involvement changed from this isolationist tone after October 2008. Rather than play a coordinating and support role through an overmatched CTF-150, the United States announced that it would stand up CTF-151, a naval task force led by a US officer and solely dedicated to combating piracy.[71] Excuses about why the US Navy could not apprehend pirates, because there was no legal system in place suitable for trying them, gave way to pragmatic negotiations with Kenya to accept accused Somali pirates. In short, the United States found a renewed willingness to become interventionist, seemingly overnight and at odds to the foot-dragging exhibited in previous months and years. With military and diplomatic mechanisms in place at the end of 2008, various officials signaled efforts to increase the US anti-piracy stance and to assume a more visible role in stopping pirate attacks.

In some instances, anti-piracy proclamations and actual events play off one another with dry comic timing. Rear Admiral Terry McKnight announced on 28 January 2009 that the recent arrival of the US-led CTF-151 had made "dramatic" inroads in the battle against piracy.[72] The next day, Somali pirates seized the German-flagged liquid petroleum tanker MV *Longchamp* in the heart of the zone CTF-151 intended to protect, marking the third ship taken in 2009.[73] Later on 29 January, a member of the media corrected Admiral McKnight's statement at a roundtable interview that "there has not been a successful pirated [*sic*] event" since CTF-151 stood up, demonstrating how intractable a problem it is to keep track of all Somali pirate attacks, let alone prevent them.[74]

---

[71] The 2008 incarnation of CTF-151 is independent from the TF-151 that had performed surveillance in the Arabian Sea as part of OEF until CTF-150 absorbed it in 2004; see Karin Junker, Michel-Ange Scarbonchi, and Fodé Sylla, "Report of the Ad Hoc Delegation of the CDC on Its Mission to Djibouti," (Brussels: European Parliament, 2004).

[72] Gregory Viscusi, "Pirate Attacks Cut Dramatically by Navies, US Admiral Says," *Bloomberg.com* (2009), http://www.bloomberg.com/apps/news?pid=20601102&sid=aXR8.j52hcpo&refer=uk (accessed 28 January 2009).

[73] "Somali Pirates Seize German Ship," *BBC News* (2009), http://news.bbc.co.uk/1/hi/world/africa/7858462.stm (accessed 30 January 2009).

[74] Terry McKnight, (Rear Admiral, US Navy; Commander, Task Force 151), Interview: Department of Defense Bloggers' Roundtable, 29 January 2009

The incident was also representative of increasing Somali pirate sophistication. According to real-time reporting from the International Chamber of Commerce (ICC) Commercial Crime Services (CCS) Live Piracy database, the *Longchamp*, on its way to Asia from Europe, was "escorted by a naval convoy when it was boarded by seven armed pirates."[75] Further reports revealed that the vessel was a victim of a decoy attack. Other pirate boats made attention-grabbing attacks against two other small ships, diverting the attention of the Indian warship protecting the convoy. As the Indian warship dispersed the attacks, a third pair of boats attacked the *Longchamp*, which has a low freeboard, was easy to board, and was apparently the intended primary target. A week later, India announced an increased commitment to maintain two warships on a continuous watch in and near the Gulf of Aden and sent the INS *Tabar* back to the region. The *Longchamp* incident provides a good illustration of how military rhetoric and actual commitment— from any nation—has not yet risen to a level able to overcome the threat of Somali piracy. This fight is a difficult one—it is worthy of a great power.

At this writing, the *Maersk Alabama* incident may move, more than any other action, the United States away from its lethargy about Somali pirates. This chapter discussed the military attention the seizure of a US ship attracted and mentioned how the incident rapidly cleared up previously thorny legal issues. More calls for a greater US anti-piracy role began to enter the Congressional Record in mid-2009.[76] The dramatic abduction and rescue of Captain Phillips has dislodged some US uncertainty about its anti-piracy role, but the question of why that uncertainty existed at all remains worthy of further discussion.

Conclusion

Somali piracy, a problem that the international maritime community recognized as growing out of control by 2005, caught the world's attention in 2008 because of its wide-ranging scope, its criminal characteristics, and the legal questions it raised. The United States, its focus scattered among other troubled areas of the globe, was hopeful that other nations would step forward to answer the growing chorus calling for action

---

[75] Commercial Crime Services, "Live Piracy Site," (International Chamber of Commerce (http://www.ics-ccs.org), 2009).

[76] Kimberly Hefling, "Senator Asks Military to Step up Pirate Patrols," *Associated Press* (2009), http://www.google.com/hostednews/ap/article/ALeqM5jDwPwVBkcirkTon7pMMfS63vhNGgD980AKBO0 (accessed 7 May 2009).

against pirates, and was willing to claim an inability to act based upon archaic maritime law. When states that challenge US interests provided this hoped-for intervention, the political economy calculus changed. The US moved quickly to establish and to take a more visible lead in anti-piracy mechanisms with greater credibility. Chapter 3 provides a framework for understanding both the initial US hesitance to act and its later growing assertiveness against piracy. This theoretical understanding is critical for describing the pertinent IR dynamics of Somali piracy and for making recommendations about future US policy.

Chapter 3

Theory: Strategic Culture and Structural Realism

States, like people, are insecure in proportion to the extent of their freedom.

—Kenneth Waltz, *Theory of International Politics*

National strategic culture and style should represent a tolerable fusion of what a society prefers and of what tends to succeed for that society.

—Colin Gray, *Explorations in Strategy*

Introduction

The previous two chapters of this thesis describe the conditions that allow piracy to thrive and demonstrate that those conditions have allowed piracy to blossom near Somalia. These chapters also claim that the battle against piracy has defined superpowers throughout history, and assert that the United States at first had appeared unwilling to take up this fight against Somali piracy. This is a bold claim, and it is helpful to establish a theoretical framework to explain this perceived reluctance. To accomplish that goal, this chapter describes two theoretical viewpoints, one from a perspective of *strategic culture* and one with a vantage of *structural realism*. The thesis asserts that these two schools of IR theory explain why the United States appeared for a time to avoid confronting piracy, even though reigning superpowers have accepted this challenge in the past.

From the beginning, it is worth noting that a conceptual chasm separates the theories of strategic culture and structural realism. The rift between the two theories appears in the divergent threads they follow in IR literature. Either strategic culture or structural realism appears as a valid theoretical lens to examine international behavior, but few authors employ both at the same time. In spite of this division, this thesis attempts to synthesize both perspectives, because together they appear to explain the recent US military response to piracy. Comparing these disparate ideas gives strategic culture a structure that it often lacks, and adds cultural nuance to otherwise inflexible structural realist explanations. This exploration begins with a description of strategic culture, briefly mentioning two competing subthemes in its body of literature. The chapter then describes structural realism and contrasts it to strategic culture.

The chapter's conclusion is that both theories benefit by borrowing from each other. The combination of both concepts in a theoretical framework gives both strategic culture, by itself an amorphous abstraction, and structural realism, on its own a rigid oversimplification, explanatory power for issues of national choice. With this theoretical background in hand, this thesis goes on to apply these concepts in chapter 4, positing a complete picture of the recent US piracy response. With piracy as a model, the thesis also makes conclusions about the role of national preferences and structural obligations in forming broader US policy. Understanding strategic culture and structural realism is essential to this analysis.

Strategic Culture

Alan Macmillan and Ken Booth define strategic culture as individual nations' approaches to "solving problems with respect to the threat or use of force."[1] This paper adopts their definition. This approach implies that strategic culture represents a nation's likelihood to use or threaten to use its military forces. Strategic culture as described here has little to say about minimum acceptable friendly-enemy force ratios, types of weapons used, or anything else typified in descriptions of a particular nation's way of war. It refers to a nation's tendency to choose military force to solve problems, but not to the specific means by which the nation applies that force after making that decision. As applied to piracy, the theory only asks whether a nation will use military forces to tackle the problem; it cannot produce a recommendation about how many ships to send.

Interventionism and isolationism are the pertinent measures of strategic culture— classifying a country with either label is the output of this theoretical construct. Interventionism is a nation's willingness to involve itself in the affairs of another. Isolationism is abstention from alliances and other international political bodies and in this study implies an unwillingness to use military force to deal with Somali piracy. In the framework offered here, the realm of possible military response to Somali piracy is almost binary: the nation either makes a military commitment to fight pirates or remains

---

[1]Macmillan and Booth, "Strategic Culture–Framework for Analysis," 363.

disengaged from the problem. In reality—and in the case of Somali piracy—available responses occupy a spectrum bounded by absolute isolationism (no ships or other military assets go to the Gulf of Aden or Indian Ocean) to extreme interventionism (US warships and troops lead an international coalition to destroy pirates on the sea and on the land). Realistic responses lie somewhere in the middle of these two extremes.[2]

As a caveat, the reader should appreciate that application of strategic culture as a concept in theoretical frameworks does not happen uniformly. Some authors, typified by Alistair Johnston, examine strategic culture as the driver of national behavior, and seek to develop and test models to see if they can really predict what a country will do in a certain situation.[3] Other authors, represented by Colin Gray, assert that attempts to isolate strategic culture this way deny the nature of culture. Culture, along with six other concepts that Gray calls the "seven contexts of war," is so pervasive in the context of strategy that efforts to isolate it doom any useful modeling effort.[4]

Recognizing this difference is helpful, as is recognition of culture's ambiguity. Anthropologist Leslie A. White points out that consensus about the definition of *culture*, even in a relatively narrow band of academic literature, does not exist: "Culture is not basically anything. Culture is a word concept. It is man-made and may be used arbitrarily to designate anything; we may define the concept as we please."[5] Appreciating this lack of consensus allows a way forward: after identifying the ways in which working definitions of strategic culture differ, one may decide what parts of existing definitions remain useful in a given model. This study identifies two main conceptualizations of strategic culture. The first is simplistic; the second is more complex.

---

[2] This choice of definition for strategic culture and the simplistic means of measuring it put helpful bounds on the research problem. A qualitative measurement of a nation's response as either preponderantly isolationist or interventionist provides a useful first order classification of national choice. If the response measured is unique to a specific problem (as it is with piracy), making this kind of subjective, binary classification frees one of the need to make detailed judgments about the characteristics of a response. On the other hand, summing several responses to a range of specific problems still allows a nuanced appreciation of whether a nation's overall behavior reflects isolationist or interventionist tendencies.
[3] The "driver" of behavior is an "independent variable" in the academic literature. See Alastair Iain Johnston, "Thinking About Strategic Culture," *International Security* 19, no. 4 (Spring 1995): 33.
[4] The seven contexts are "political, social-cultural, economic, technological, military-strategic, geopolitical and geostrategic, and historical." See Colin S. Gray, *Fighting Talk: Forty Maxims on War, Peace, and Strategy* (Westport, CT: Praeger Security International, 2007), 3.
[5] Leslie A. White, *The Concept of Cultural Systems: A Key to Understanding Tribes and Nations* (New York: Columbia University Press, 1975), 4n.

Simple Models of Strategic Culture

In general, authors who think that strategic culture can predict national behavior share two common tendencies. First, these authors relate strategic culture to a less abstract variable or combination of variables that is easy to quantify or qualify. This simplistic approach invites criticism from other authors. Alan Bloomfield and Kim Richard Nossal review authors who cite "causes" of state behavior including technology, demography, economic development, and geography.[6] They go on to criticize Johnston's use of culture as definitively shaping strategic behavior, specifically because he uses a definition of culture that does not include behavior. Johnston's motivation for excluding behavior in the definition of culture is to allow him to make behavior the dependent variable in his model—he seeks to explain behavior as a response to inputs shaped by a kind of cultural filter. To make his model work, Johnston defines culture in terms of other abstractions, namely "argumentation structures, languages, analogies, [and] metaphors," and his approach typifies a simplistic definition of strategic culture.[7]

Theorists like Johnston may make simple links between these abstractions and culture, but they draw complicated conclusions about the character of strategic culture. The second tendency of authors who attempt to reduce strategic culture to an independent variable is to conclude that other forces can easily reshape a nation's strategic culture. As an example, Oliver Lee describes the development of strategic culture in the light of geography, which is a strategic variable that changes slowly at best. He concludes that fluctuating democratic control of American foreign policy shapes strategic culture. At times, elite groups motivated by the idea of free trade control foreign policy. These groups tend to be zealously interventionist in their approach to IR. On the other hand, Lee feels that other elite coalitions drive US foreign policy toward its natural bent, which is geographically determined isolationism.[8] In both situations, the important point is that the opinions of governing elites shape the strategic culture.

Jeffrey Lantis, discussing German strategic culture vis-à-vis its involvement in the 1998 Kosovo crisis, concludes, "Evolution of strategic culture may be more abrupt, less

---

[6] Alan Bloomfield and Kim Richard Nossal, "Towards an Explicative Understanding of Strategic Culture: The Cases of Australia and Canada," *Contemporary Security Policy* 28, no. 2 (August 2007): 286.

[7] Bloomfield and Nossal, "Towards an Explicative Understanding of Strategic Culture: The Cases of Australia and Canada," 287.

[8] Oliver Lee, "The Geopolitics of America's Strategic Culture," *Comparative Strategy* 27, no. 3 (2008).

difficult, and more prevalent than traditional scholarship seems to allow."[9] Johnston arrives at a similar conclusion, arguing, "Leadership change, elite transformation, bureaucratic politics, technology cycles, internal debates, or external crisis might cause a certain strategic culture to emerge dominant."[10] As with Lee's assessment, these views of strategic culture make it a function of opinions held by elites—the central idea here is that strategic culture can vary as quickly as political cycles change.

Complex Models of Strategic Culture

The belief that strategic culture changes quickly as elites coalesce and diverge is not universal. Michael Evans writes that Australia's island geography has led to a consistent strategic culture impervious to changing world situations or opinions.[11] For Evans, Australia's inward looking, continental viewpoint keeps it from developing a realistic perception of its ocean dependence in a globalized world, even if some elites do realize how important sea trade is to Australia and would like to change its strategic culture. Evans' theory implies that variables like geography rigidly determine strategic culture, but his ideas about the way geography molds strategic culture echo Colin Gray, who advocates a complex approach to the concept. For Gray, strategic culture is less subject to change over time—"it is not going to yield readily, painlessly, and comprehensively to a would-be revolutionary drive from the policymakers of the moment"—its meaning is broader, enduring, and inseparable from the other strategic contexts he identifies.[12]

Unlike Johnston, Gray rejects models that promise to make culture a falsifiable, independent variable. Gray argues against this approach with some passion.[13] He also argues that strategic culture has an enduring character, one that is not as subject to influence of the opinions of elites. Strategic culture can and does vary with time, as do other strategic contexts, but it is not a conscious choice subject to change as quickly as

---

[9] Jeffrey Lantis, "The Moral Imperative of Force: The Evolution of German Strategic Culture in Kosovo," *Comparative Strategy* 21, no. 1 (2002): 40.

[10] Johnston, "Thinking About Strategic Culture," 53.

[11] Michael Evans, "Island-Consciousness and Australian Strategic Culture," *Institute of Public Affairs Review* 58, no. 2 (July 2006).

[12] Colin S. Gray, "Out of the Wilderness: Prime Time for Strategic Culture," *Comparative Strategy* 26, no. 1 (2007): 12.

[13] In addition: "Scholarship on strategic culture…similarly is bound to fail when it…positivistically seeks a certain general wisdom." See Gray, "Out of the Wilderness," 1.

human opinions. Along with his claim that strategic culture is not subject to rapid change, Gray is committed to the idea that one cannot describe it in detail. In his own words, "claims of an essentialist kind (the United States is *really*...) lean upon strategic cultural assertions that typically escape disciplined evaluation."[14] Here is a summary of the resulting dichotomy: authors like Johnston provide a simplified picture of strategic culture and believe that it changes quickly with the opinions of political elites; authors like Gray insist on a complex concept of strategic culture and believe that the phenomenon remains more or less constant over time.

Common Concepts of Strategic Culture

After highlighting these differences among theorists who favor strategic culture as a lens for examining national behavior, it is useful to point out what they have in common. The first shared idea is that strategic culture links to other measurable national characteristics. Even as Gray has gone to great lengths to comment unfavorably on authors favoring rigid models of strategic culture, like Johnston, his analyses reveal that he also links strategic culture to simple underlying causes. Gray argues that important constants like geography, though they do not directly determine strategic culture, influence it in important ways. He states as a maxim that "all strategy is geostrategy: geography is fundamental."[15] Inasmuch as there is a link between strategic culture and strategy, this line of argument seems to put him in good company with Lee, albeit with different ramifications.[16]

The second idea repeated by both main types of strategic culture theorists is the idea that strategic culture can and does change over time. There are differences in time horizon and mechanics for different camps, but neither set holds that strategic culture remains static. Johnston argues that culture changes relatively quickly as elite opinions change; Gray believes that less malleable underlying factors shape strategic culture but acknowledges, "Strategic cultures are constantly being altered as succeeding generations of strategic thinkers reinterpret the past."[17] If strategic culture is ultimately about the

---

[14] Colin S. Gray, *Explorations in Strategy* (Westport, CT: Praeger, 1996), 85, italics in original.
[15] Gray, *Fighting Talk*, 78.
[16] Where Lee argues that Australia's island geography makes it inward looking and circumspect in the use of military force, Gray argues that the same island geography causes the United States to be more reliant on airpower, and hence more likely to take interventionist actions.
[17] Colin S. Gray, *Modern Strategy* (Oxford: Oxford University Press, 1999), 81.

willingness to use force in solving IR problems, realizing that it changes cyclically suggests a schematic like the one shown in figure 3. The sinusoidal curve associated with country A simply illustrates the possibility of national preference to vary over time. Few countries are likely to ricochet between extremes like this—or to swing with the same kind of periodicity. Country B's line imagines a country with interventionist tendencies that for some reason abandons that approach to become somewhat isolationist. Country C's line depicts a slightly isolationist bent, but at times the strategic culture favors a marked increase in interventionism. At times countries appear interventionist, eager to be involved in many international affairs; at other times isolationism seems to carry the day, with a country looking for reasons to keep to itself. The shape of the curve varies for each nation, and is visible only with strategic hindsight.

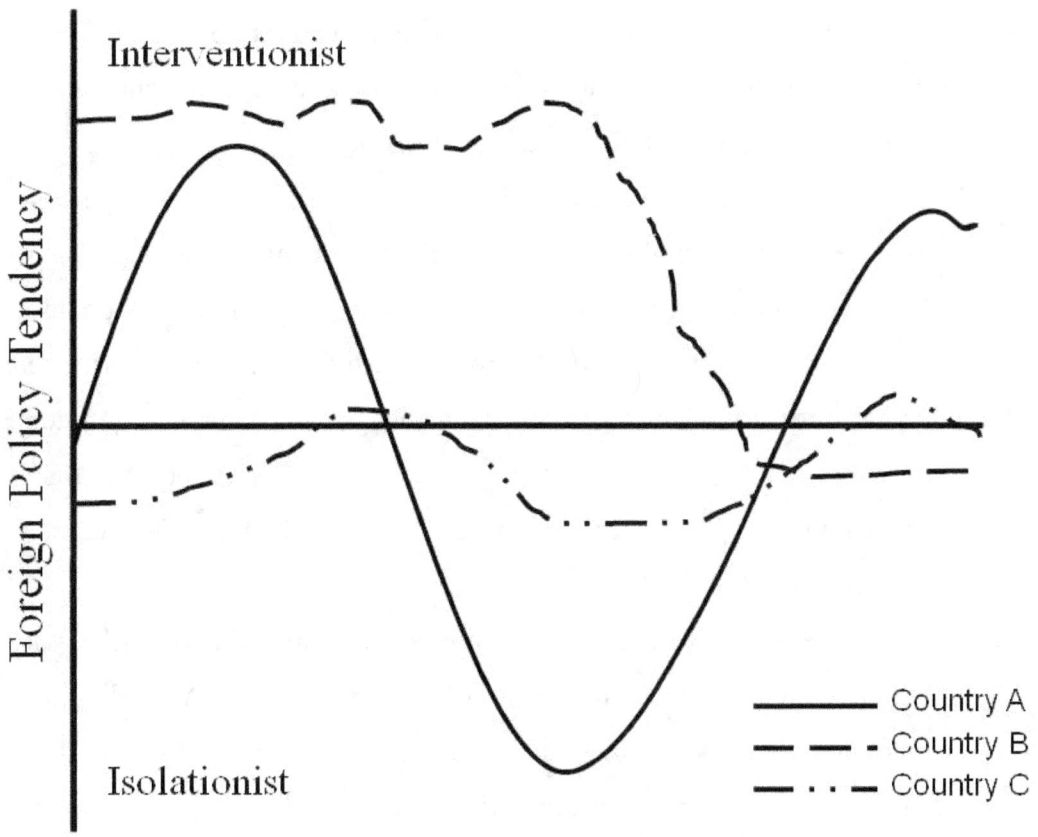

Figure 3: Strategic cultural tendencies
Source: Author's original work

A third common theme among strategic culture scholars is the view that strategic culture emerges as a summation of other internal factors. Lee views strategic culture as a combination of perceived geopolitical possibilities and a country's potential in the international environment.[18] Gray, in contrast, sees culture instead as a combination of history and geography.[19] Bloomfield and Nossal examine ideational, material, and behavioral elements in explaining a given nation's strategic culture.[20] Many authors point out that factors tending to result in isolationism are cultural constants with long-standing historical antecedents, whereas interventionist factors ebb and flow more frequently at the whim of prevailing political attitudes. The common ground here does not imply that all strategic culture authors agree on the relevant elements. As mentioned above, their disagreements tend to be vociferous. The most important consequence, though, is that all these authors identify the impact of internal politics on a nation's international behavior.

The fourth piece of common ground among strategic culture authors is the idea of free national choice. For authors like Johnston and Lee, free choice exists when IR elites choose a particular strategic posture that the nation follows. For authors like Gray and Evans, it is a nation's freedom from the constraints of an international system. In other words, although several factors might influence a nation's strategic culture, the behavior of other nations in the context of an international system does not determine national behavior. Gray, who ardently defends the idea that national security behavior is a domestic decision, does not do so to distance himself from other strategic culturalists with whom he disagrees on certain points. Rather, his target is theorists with a drastically different view of IR: those who explain it through the lens of structural realism.[21]

Structural Realism

The basic concept of structural realism is simple to describe, particularly in contrast with the nuanced intricacies of strategic culture. According to Kenneth Waltz, a cornerstone of the structural realist school, structural realism views the world as an anarchic system containing states who act in their own interests to maintain a constant

---

[18] Lee, "The Geopolitics of America's Strategic Culture," 269.
[19] Gray, "Out of the Wilderness," 5.
[20] Bloomfield and Nossal, "Towards an Explicative Understanding of Strategic Culture: The Cases of Australia and Canada," 304.
[21] Gray's contempt is unmistakable: "So the neorealist proposition that strategic history, past, present, and future, can be explained strictly by reference to the relations among political entities, with no regard paid to their domestic processes, is, frankly, preposterous." See Gray, "Out of the Wilderness," 6.

balance of power.[22] The theory, like strategic culture, deals with the use of force, finding mankind's widespread use of force to be proof for and the defining characteristic of an anarchic world. Proceeding from an argument that only states have a legitimate right to use force against each other (in contrast to individuals, who do so illegitimately), Waltz finds the international system to be one of anarchy characterized by nations' use of force for the purposes of self-help.[23] The behavior of the Somali pirates is a good metaphor for the structural realist view of the world. In an anarchic world (the absence of an effective Somali government), the pirates use force (seizing ships) for self-help (to make a living and become wealthy).

The anarchic nature of the international system limits options of its participants in two ways. First, though nations are interdependent and would benefit from a comparative advantage via increased specialization, becoming overly specialized makes a nation vulnerable to exploitation by another. Second, although it is inefficient for all nations to do so, each spends a certain amount of its wealth ensuring that other states cannot attack it with impunity.[24] In general, nation-states face a constant dilemma: many of the things they do for national survival benefit neither the world at large nor their own long-term interests, yet they must do them anyway to ensure survival.[25]

In describing strategic culture, this paper defined isolationism and interventionism in terms of national choice—a state could elect to become or not become involved in international affairs. In the logic of structural realism, the element of choice, if not completely removed, is severely constrained. Because structural realism implies that states *must* act whenever the balance of power shifts, isolationism in a realist theoretical structure implies either a lack of overlapping interests or relative structural weakness. In other words, a state behaves in an isolationist way when it can neither gain from nor lose by a given action, or would only further reduce its relative power if it did get involved. Interventionism implies that interests overlap and that a state acts from a position of relative strength. Involvement in a matter offers an increase in or maintenance of relative

[22] Kenneth N. Waltz, "Structural Realism after the Cold War," *International Security* 25, no. 1 (Summer 2000): 5.
[23] Kenneth N. Waltz, *Theory of International Politics* (New York: McGraw-Hill, Inc., 1979), 103.
[24] Waltz, *Theory of International Politics*, 104–07.
[25] Waltz, "Structural Realism after the Cold War," 24–25.

power to a state, and refusal to become involved threatens to change the overall balance of power such that the state in question might lose its relative standing.

The structural realist approach is different from the strategic cultural approach. Waltz makes assumptions about international behavior the same way economists describe individuals' microeconomic choices, and argues that aggregate international behavior reflects balanced national interests in the same way that macroeconomics accounts for the choices of many individuals.[26] These assumptions include, among other things, that nations are perfect rational actors, all subscribing to the same framework of rationality. This is the "structure" in structural realism. If that assumption is true, most choices about national use of power become foregone conclusions—in economic terms, there is always potential for profit or loss in responding to or not responding to a set of circumstances. Since nations act to maximize power gains (the same way that economic actors maximize profit) and to minimize power losses (just as economic decisions minimize economic loss), choice in most circumstances is an illusion.[27]

With the above summary of structural realism, one may compare its characteristics to the four characteristics common to strategic culture. First, with regard to links between national characteristics and national behavior, there are also implied links within the framework of structural realism, but these links differ in nature. For strategic culturalists, characteristics such as geography or the value systems of ruling elites shape national behavior. For structural realists, the arbiter of behavior is a nation's discrete standing within the existing balance of power. For a country like the United States, its response to a given security issue stems from its place in the global balance of power, its capability to act in that framework, and its relative advantages gained or lost through decisions made. For an issue like piracy, US response relates to national characteristics not through geography or culture, but through capability (the opportunity to take military action) and potential cost (power gained or lost by taking or refusing to take military action). In this framework, Australia or Lithuania would respond to piracy differently than the United States not because those countries have different strategic cultures, but because they occupy different tiers of an imagined global balance of power

---

[26] Waltz, *Theory of International Politics*, 110.

[27] Robert Heilbroner and Lester Thurow, *Economics Explained: Everything You Need to Know About How the Economy Works and Where It's Going*, 1998 ed. (New York: Touchstone, 1982), 30.

structure, which limits their range of military response options. As posited by Waltz, structural realism incorporates an acknowledgment of free riders, acknowledging the "*surprising tendency for the 'exploitation' of the great by the small*," and he advocates for small numbers (ideally two) of great powers.[28]

The second area of comparison is the potential for change. Although strategic culturalists disagree on the precise mechanisms and kinetic rates, all concede that strategic culture may change over time. For structural realists, change of one kind or another happens frequently, but the type of change is qualitatively different than that with which culturalists contemplate. For Waltz, "within-system" changes can be relatively small (such as means of transportation or communication) or large (such as development of nuclear weapons or changing from a bipolar to multipolar world). Small changes happen frequently; large changes happen less often, but do occur. Of the world's systemic characteristics of "anarchy, self-help, and power balancing" upon which Waltz built his theory of structural realism, he concedes no changes, no matter the opinion of certain policy elites.[29] Failing to maximize national power would be to behave irrationally.

Strategic culturalist authors recognize that strategic culture is a summation of other national characteristics. As a third comparison, this idea is lacking in structural realism, where power is the only pertinent independent variable. The neglect of structural realism's accommodation for the unique internal aspects of participants in the international system is the culturalists' main critique of the system.[30] Again, the sums that structural realism calculates are of a different type. Waltz concerns himself with fungible economic, population, and military indicators that indicate measures of power of nations relative to each other.[31] He does not pay regard to cultural or other internal considerations that affect the way nations employ the trappings of power at their disposal.

The first three comparisons shape and lead to the fourth. The absence of choice is the most glaring and significant difference between strategic culture and structural

---

[28] Mancur Olson, *The Logic of Collective Action: Public Goods and the Theory of Groups*, 1971 ed. (Cambridge, MA: Harvard University Press, 1965), 35. The quotation and advocacy for a bipolar world appear in Waltz, *Theory of International Politics*, 208–10, italics in original.
[29] Waltz, "Structural Realism after the Cold War," 5–6.
[30] Gray, "Out of the Wilderness," 6.
[31] Waltz, *Theory of International Politics*, 212–22.

realism. Of the other common themes central to strategic culture—links to internal national characteristics, potential to change over time, and a summation of other variables—in the matter of choice alone is there no middle ground. From a vantage of strategic culture, nations choose to a degree whether to be interventionist or isolationist with respect to certain matters. In the structural realist lens, nations have no choice: they must at all times be self-interested and act to maximize power in the confines of an anarchic system.[32] In the world's tightly woven and interdependent *realpolitik* structure, some national "choices" are ineluctable outcomes, tailored responses to the actions of other nations in the context of the existing world power balance. In a bipolar world, structural realism suggests a model of two point forces influencing each other to maintain a constant balance of power between two competing powers, as in figure 4.

---

[32] This is the approach of basic structural realism. Other authors, including Waltz, acknowledge that other factors, including geography, national politics, and specific types of power imbalance, can have complicating effects on the balance of power calculus. See, for example, Emerson M.S. Niou, Peter C. Ordeshook, and Gregory F. Rose, *The Balance of Power: Stability in International Systems* (Cambridge: Cambridge University Press, 1989), 312–13.

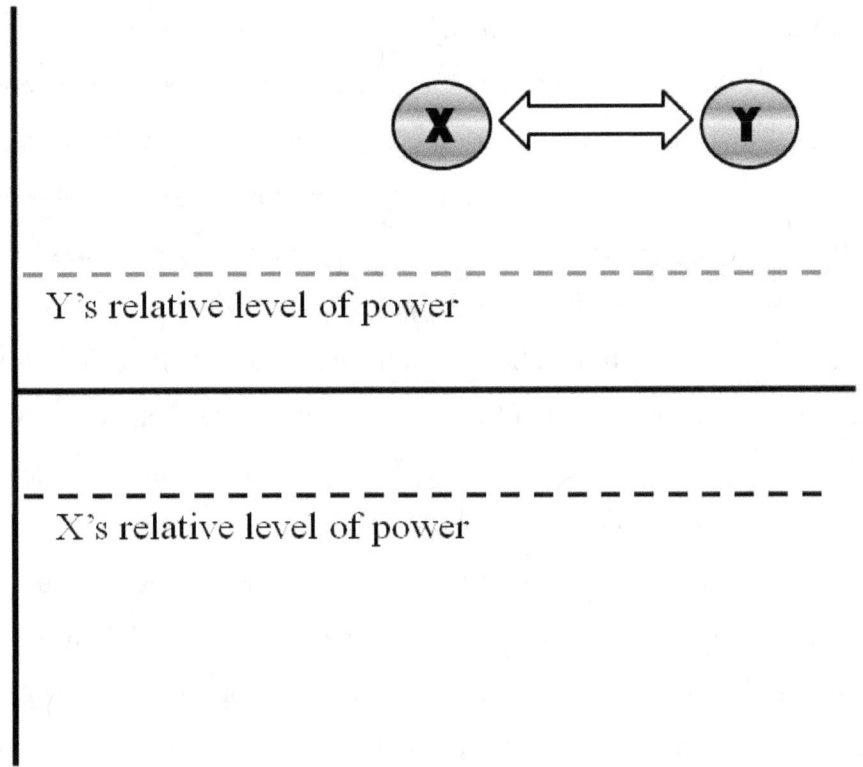

Figure 4. Structural imperatives
Source: Author's original work

Combining Theories?

Just as strong governments and piracy seldom cohabitate, it is rare to find both strategic culture and structural realism discussed alongside each other in IR literature. Some authors make their reasons for this clear. Colin Gray is not charitable in his assessment of structural realism, finding it "so absurd that no one would, or should, take it seriously."[33] He believes that simple balance-of-power calculations, independent of a nation's internal context, do not explain national behavior. Alastair Johnston is more tactful, but his description of his scholarship stresses that it is an effort to separate culture from the "ahistorical, non-cultural neorealist framework for analyzing strategic choices."[34] He argues that making study of strategic culture useful requires limiting the number of "relevant explanatory variables" that combine to create the strategic culture in

---

[33] Gray, "Out of the Wilderness," 6.
[34] Johnston, "Thinking About Strategic Culture," 35.

question.[35] He separates national behavior from culture with caution in order to examine culture as an independent variable affecting national behavior.

Gray will not concede any such separation, even a cautious one. This thesis recognizes that Gray and Johnston approach the concept of strategic culture from different perspectives. The more parsimonious conclusions of Johnston allow one to reconcile strategic culture with structural realism, but Gray's ideas have enduring merit as well and are worth retaining. For the purposes of trying to marry strategic culture with structural realism, Johnston allows that the existence of strategic culture "implies that a state's strategic behavior is not fully responsive to others' choices," without hewing rigidly to Gray's implication, rooted in his rejection of structural realism, that state behavior is *never* responsive to other's choices.[36]

The structure offered by Waltz's theory gives strategic culture explanatory power. Without structure, strategic culture is too unbounded to explain much. With White's realization that "culture is not basically anything" hanging in the void, a reader quickly sees that culture on its own does not predict national behavior. Since it can cover a range of behaviors that range from the opinions expressed by elites to war-fighting habits, ideas about strategic culture are too malleable to have explanatory power.

Structural realism suffers from its own flaws. Although its proponents present evidence that international behavior constitutes a balancing act in an anarchic environment, the entire theory strains belief by not acknowledging internal national politics at all. As Emerson Niou, Peter Ordeshook, and Gregory Rose argue, one "cannot ignore 'mundane' domestic concerns."[37] One must also acknowledge an inability to calculate the precise balance of power in the world at any given time; it is an unwieldy combination of factors. Although the literature does not reveal as much diatribe from the realist school toward the culturalists as the culturalists (mostly Gray) hurl at the realists, pervasive silence implies academic contempt.

This obdurateness is unfortunate, because the middle ground is a good place to look for explanation. John Schmitt, a complexity theorist, promises that understanding a

---

[35] Johnston, "Thinking About Strategic Culture," 33.
[36] Johnston, "Thinking About Strategic Culture," 34.
[37] Niou, Ordeshook, and Rose, *The Balance of Power*, 10.

problem well makes a solution self-evident.[38] His insinuation that self-evident solutions to wicked problems might exist at all strains belief. On the other hand, dismissing theoretical structures that have proven explanatory power is to prevent effective formulation of those wicked problems, and keeps strategy out of reach. Gray may prefer enduring ambiguity to a particular model's demonstrable failure, but refusing to attempt a meaningful model will not improve anyone's ability to formulate strategy.[39] Johnston may believe the direct influence of culture is a testable proposition, but certainty in explanation or confidence in prediction is unlikely using either kind of model. An approach that accommodates both models in exposition of IR is the best approach.

Figure 5 offers a possible combination of both models. Since the combined model explains both cultural choice and structural imperatives, the graph's ordinal axis represents both preference and behavior, each described along a spectrum ranging from isolationist to interventionist. The dashed sinusoidal curve represents the fluctuating desires of a given nation's strategic culture, echoing country A from figure 1. The two dashed horizontal lines represent limits on national choice that structural realism implies. In contrast to figure 4, figure 5 considers only one country, so only one set of constraints appears. The structural constraints in figure 5 appear as a range—the area between the two lines—and represent that the realities of the world's power balance are not strictly quantum in nature (that is, figure 5's range has more possible values than figure 4's set-value lines). Instead, cognitive uncertainty (Waltz's "miscalculation" and "overreaction") and the ego of individual leaders influence the actual responses observed.[40]

---

[38] John F. Schmitt, "A Systemic Concept for Operational Design," (2006).

[39] In view of Gray's determination to keep context ambiguous, it is ironic that he insists on "decisive victory" as an achievable goal. See Colin S. Gray, "Defining and Achieving Decisive Victory," (Carlisle, PA: Strategic Studies Institute, April 2002).

[40] Waltz identifies miscalculation as the chief danger in a multipolar world, overreaction the most dangerous in a bipolar world. See Waltz, *Theory of International Politics*, 172.

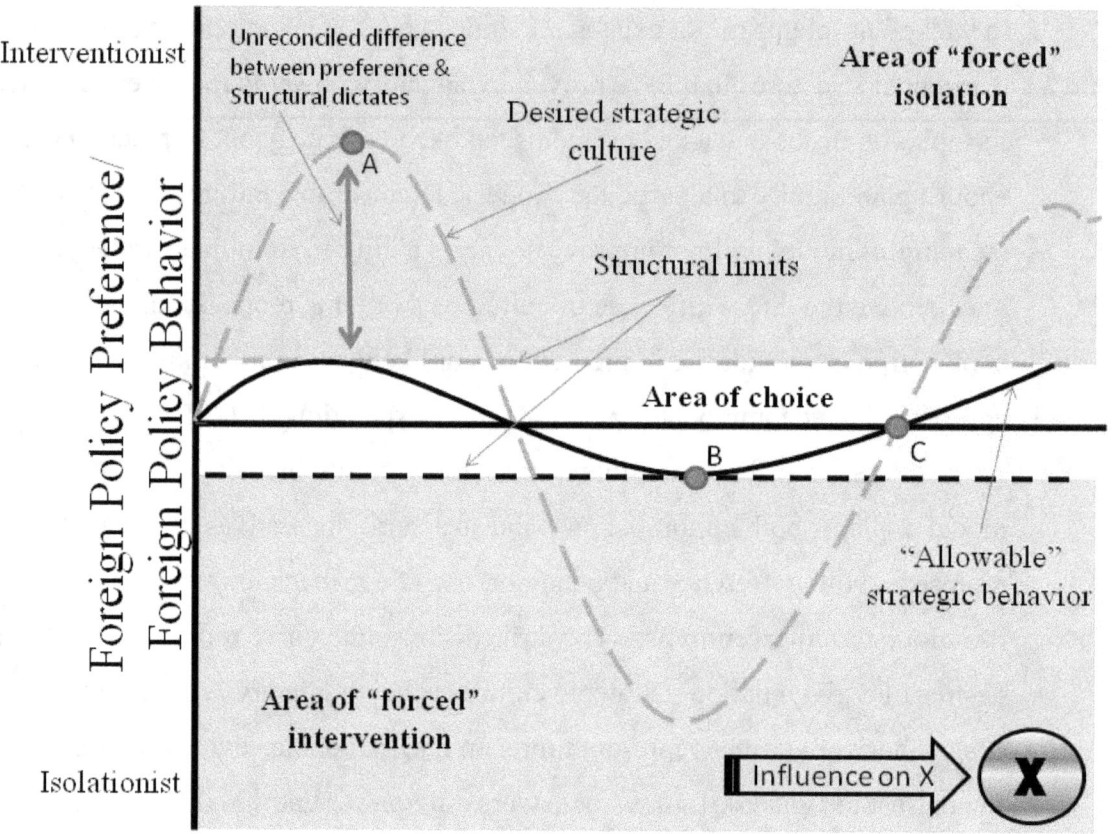

Figure 5. A Combined Model
Source: Author's original work

Within the bounds of the structural limitations is an area of choice; nations may select actions that are interventionist or isolationist consistent with their prevailing strategic cultures. Beyond this limit, though, structural considerations become paramount, and limit the effect of strategic culture on national behavior, or conversely, limit how far along the spectrum strategic culture can develop. The result is the shaded areas of the plot, which can include both isolationist and interventionist actions that are not consistent with the desired strategic culture of a nation. This representation applied to the use of military force is consistent with Richard Rosecrance's assertion that "the balance of power mechanism [does] not prevent military contests, but it [does] prevent them from getting out of hand."[41]

---

[41] Richard N. Rosecrance, *Action and Reaction in World Politics* (Boston: Little, Brown Co., 1963), 30.

A few illustrative points round out the explanation of figure 5. Point A represents a nation who does not acknowledge that its strategic cultural preference for a high degree of interventionism is limited by structural constraints calling for a more isolationist approach. A country in that situation has two choices. Adhering to structural dictates, it may make its behavior more isolationist than its cultural preferences would suggest and so avoid a loss of power within the international system. Alternatively, the country may behave outside the structural bounds—remaining more interventionist than the structural arrangement suggests. The nation may expect to lose a commensurate amount of influence, likely because of overreach in this example. Point B represents a country that has already reconciled its strategic cultural desire to withdraw from world events with the structural imperative to remain involved. It behaves in a more interventionist manner than its elites would like, but it will not lose international influence. Point C represents a country whose strategic cultural preference aligns with its structural obligations. It does not need to change its strategic behavior, and its prevailing strategic elites are content; they do not perceive dissonance between their preferences and the world's demands.

Conclusion

In combination, structural realism and strategic culture reveal mutual utility. Some nations take actions that differ from or are lesser in magnitude than an expected or expressed strategic culture—structural realist limits are in view. At the same time, national response to world events certainly derives its initial direction from strategic culture—structural realism does not hold sway at the minutest levels of detail. The action of any nation that chooses to respond to another nation's behavior reveals a measurable aspect of its strategic culture. Allowing for fluctuating national cultural preferences, a nation that responds to external events in a manner consistent with its level of power in the world and role in the international system will maintain the relative level of power it previously enjoyed. In contrast, a nation unwilling or unable to reconcile any differences between preference and structural constraint will see its level of power change. Given that world power is a zero-sum proposition and that other rational actors seek to maximize their advantages, the change will be a loss.

With the theoretical groundwork done, the next chapter will apply this analysis to the US response to Somali piracy. As chapter 2 alludes, the United States appears to have had difficulty reconciling its cultural preference for isolationism to its structural imperative as a superpower to act against piracy. The measurable characteristic, represented in figure 5 as the interface between the area of choice and the areas of mandatory action or inaction, is a *threshold of response*, and is the centerpiece of analysis for the US military response to Somali piracy in chapter 4.

Chapter 4

Synthesis and Conclusions

Months or years from now, when Somali piracy is a distant memory, its most enduring legacy will not be the spike it produced in maritime crime, or millions of dollars in ransoms paid by shipping firms and insurance companies. Instead, the piracy along the East African coast will be recalled as the catalyst for the rising navies of India, China, and the European Union to deploy far from their homeports, altering who and where they fight.

—Brian Wilson and James Kraska, *YaleGlobal,* 13 January 2009

Introduction

Building upon the historical picture of piracy, the description of contemporary Somali piracy, and the theoretical framework for understanding the use of military force provided by earlier chapters, this chapter derives lessons from the US military response to the problem of Somali piracy. The overall conclusion is that the United States in the early twenty-first century found its strategic cultural preference at odds with a structural demand for superpower action against rampant piracy. Rather than provide a meaningful and visible military response to piracy, the United States chose instead to remain part of a relatively weak international coalition against piracy. This situation changed in late 2008: US commitment to anti-piracy efforts increased after rival nations began to take the issue of piracy seriously and to send their own naval forces to the east coast of Africa. At this writing, US policy appears to have turned another corner—it has assumed a leadership role in both military and legal prosecution of piracy—following the brief capture of a US ship and longer abduction of its captain.

Using the theoretical ideas developed in chapter 3, the first part of this chapter explains the US response to piracy near Somalia. The initial reluctant US response reflected an isolationist strategic cultural preference. Structural obligations brought about a more vigorous response in late 2008 and 2009. After describing this shift in policy and the reasons behind it, the analysis concludes that tension between cultural preferences and structural imperatives shaped a tempered military response that by mid-2009 was

66

worthy of a superpower. US leadership in military operations and international law became prominent, but not excessively interventionist.

Broader lessons about strategy and hegemony fall from this analysis of piracy. As chapter 3 asserted, failing to reconcile structural imperatives at odds with cultural preferences may reduce national power. Presently, the United States seems to have resolved an initial imbalance between isolationist cultural preferences and interventionist structural imperatives in the case of piracy. Striking this kind of balance, however, is never a foregone conclusion—the United States will again face IR situations where its preferences do not align with *realpolitik* demands. An anticipation of this tension can help a nation make better decisions about the employment of its power. This chapter attempts to anticipate potential imbalances and offer appropriate recommendations for groups involved in the employment of national power.

Changing US Responses to Piracy: Achieving Cultural-Structural Equilibrium

A short article in the March 2009 issue of *Navy Times* serves as a synopsis of the change in US policy toward Somali piracy. In describing CTF-151's newest flagship, the USS *Boxer*, the article states, "CTF-151 stood up in January following a rapid spike in pirate attacks off the coast of Somalia and in the Gulf of Aden that began in August. It originally was made up of US forces, but naval forces from the United Kingdom, Denmark, and Turkey now participate."[1]

The above two sentences beg clarification. To begin, the spike in piracy attacks mentioned as beginning in August is a debatable matter. August 2008 certainly did not bring the first evidence that piracy was surging near Somalia. The November 2005 attack against the cruise ship *Seabourn Spirit* more than 100 miles off the Somali coast sent a clear message about the capability of pirates there. Among other things, it showed that pirate gangs employed the use of "motherships," used advanced weapons, including rocket-propelled grenades, and possessed the ability to strike well beyond the coastal range Western nations had previously assumed.[2]

---

[1] "Boxer Becomes Piracy Task Force Flagship," *Navy Times* (2009), http://www.navytimes.com/news/2009/03/navy_flagship151_031009/ (accessed 11 March 2009).

[2] A mothership is a larger fishing vessel that does not attack ships itself but rather serves as staging areas for smaller pirate attack vessels. See Matt Cherry and Amanda Moyer, "US Navy Boards Ship after Pirate Attack," *CNN.com* (2005), http://www.cnn.com/2005/WORLD/africa/11/07/somalia.pirates/index.html (accessed 2 April 2009).

Setting this issue of timing aside, the response time of five months is much longer than the US Navy needs to create a task force.[3] The delay instead reflects a conscious decision to stay out of this particular international concern. The second sentence of the *Navy Times* article quoted above implies that European partners have joined a US-led effort, which is only partly true. European nations that had been combating piracy as part of an effort encouraged by the United States have continued to do so, with many increasing their commitment throughout 2008. European efforts included collaborating with US operations, but an independent operation also received wide support. Operation Atalanta, the European Union effort announced in mid-December, is an excellent example of third-party involvement that the United States seemed to have been encouraging before an additional and solely US effort went forward in early 2009.[4] The timeline in figure 6 displays significant piracy events, policy announcements, and international military commitments pertaining to Somali piracy in 2008 and 2009.

---

[3] Anthony J. Linardi, (Commander, US Navy), in discussion with the author, 2 April 2009.
[4] CTF-151 started with three ships, and all were US vessels. Since then, it has incorporated international partners; see McKnight, roundtable interview, 29 January 2009.

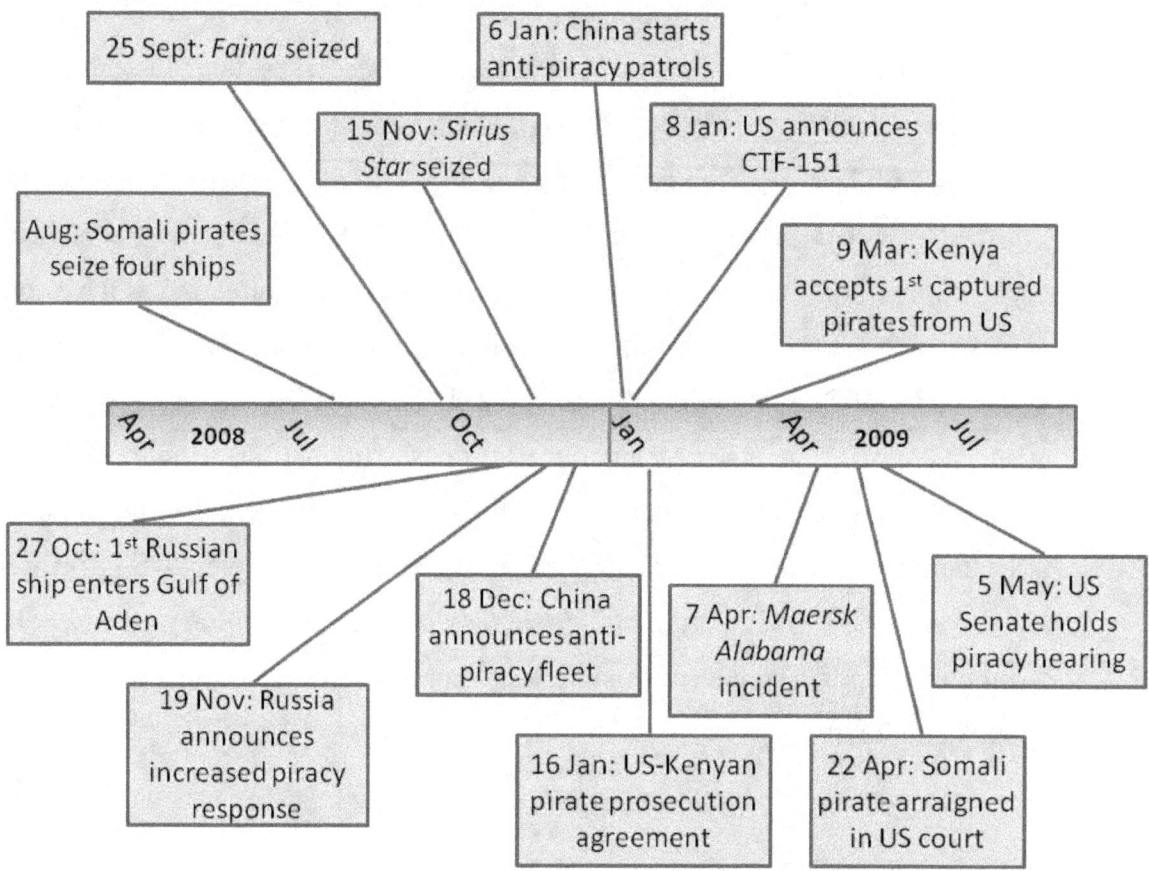

Figure 6: Timeline of US and rival anti-piracy involvement
Source: Author's original work

The timeline highlights two observations. First, piracy, already a years-old problem for shipping near Somalia, leapt into significant press attention again as early as August 2008. Second, while the US military response clearly lags both significant piracy events as well as the military actions of rival nations, the response embodied in CTF-151's stand-up is a clear response to the latter. Following months of public encouragement for multilateral response to the Somali piracy issue and diplomatic foot-dragging on the legal disposition of captured pirates, the United States in a manner of days stood up a naval task force and negotiated a quick diplomatic agreement for a prosecution venue, signaling serious intent to interdict pirates.

In agreement with the *Navy Times* article quoted at the beginning of this chapter, media summaries of these actions suggest that they are a response to "a rapid spike in pirate attacks." This thesis argues otherwise. Instead, the desired strategic culture of the United States, as shaped by policy elites, was one polarized toward isolationism even though Somali piracy had years ago reached levels unacceptable to an open world trade regime. This isolationist tendency, revealed in signals sent by the US in its contemporary response to piracy, abruptly changed at the end of 2008. The argument is that piracy, no more or less significant to US interests in 2008 than before, created other strategic circumstances that the United States could not ignore. Namely, rival nations' military responses to piracy created structural constraints that limited the United States' desired isolationist response. In mid-2009, the US response to piracy grew stronger: a captured Somali pirate faced trial in New York, the US Senate held a hearing on piracy, and several nations followed the US lead of having captured pirates prosecuted in Kenya.[5]

This thesis argues that the increased response is an appropriate development. The isolationist preferences of IR elites to mute the US response to piracy wrestled with the enduring historic demand that superpowers lead the way in battling pirates. The ensuing result was a policy that maintained the US role as a respected defender of freedom of the seas while it avoided charges of either negligence or over-involvement. This section traces the development of the US response to piracy, highlighting the cultural and structural forces that shaped the observed mid-2009 policy.

Initial Response: Desired Isolationism

There are several *prima facie* reasons to deduce that the preferred strategic posture of the United States to international piracy in the early twenty-first century would be one of isolationism. First, US military involvement in wars of choice since 2003 was at a high level compared to other episodes in history. Bruce Jentleson argues that US popular patience for conflict is much stronger when the conflict appears as restraint of an aggressor nation; patience is scant when the conflict appears to be an effort to change a government.[6] The operations in Iraq from 2003 and Afghanistan from 2001 fit the latter description.

Second, the signals of IR elites, both in general and with specific regard to Somali piracy, indicated no significant desire to engage the problem. As an example of general isolationist bent, comments from the incoming Obama administration showed that

---

[5] "French Hand over 11 Suspected Pirates to Kenya," *Associated Press* (8 May 2009), http://www.google.com/hostednews/ap/article/ALeqM5gB7YMEDuCwwY9ncDOtPAkEI4-H2wD9824F680 (accessed 24 May 2009).
[6] Bruce W. Jentleson, "The Pretty Prudent Public: Post Post-Vietnam American Opinion on the Use of Military Force," *International Studies Quarterly* 36, no. 1 (March 1992): 49.

concepts from Joseph Nye's *Soft Power* figured with prominence in the playbooks of American diplomacy. Nye's manifesto calls for policies "consistent with democracy, human rights, *openness*, and respect for the opinions of others" that eschew "arrogance."[7] The first executive orders signed by President Obama hewed closely to this line of thinking, mandating openness with information for government agencies in the name of making "transparency and rule of law...the touchstones of this presidency."[8] Implicit in rhetoric like this is the idea that the United States will not seek further theaters for military involvement around the world. Reflecting the ideological bent of the Obama administration and reluctance to lead in military affairs, US Secretary of State Hillary Clinton repeated as a mantra that the United States sought international cooperation to stop piracy.[9]

Senior military leaders' comments about strategic exhaustion, discussed in chapter 3, express isolationist preferences for an organization charged with fighting the nation's battles. On one hand, the remarks may simply reflect the professional military's "cautious, conservative, restraining voice to the formation of state policy" that Samuel Huntington described.[10] On the other, these remarks may make it more difficult for political leaders to commit military force to situations requiring the use of force. To the degree that military preference reflects a strategic cultural preference at odds with structural imperatives, these messages embody the worst possible outcome of the Powell Doctrine that Eliot Cohen criticizes: national leaders are unable to employ, unhindered, a

---

[7] Joseph S. Nye, *Soft Power: The Means to Success in World Politics* (Cambridge, MA: Perseus Books Group, 2004), 32 (emphasis added).

[8] Sheryl Gay Stolberg, "On First Day, Obama Quickly Sets a New Tone," *The New York Times*, 21 January 2009, A1.

[9] During the *Maersk Alabama* situation, Secretary Clinton made a prominent call for more countries to fight Somali piracy. Making such a request while attempting to free a US citizen from pirate captors does not explicitly signal the notion that the United States cannot sufficiently protect its own interests, but that is a possible interpretation. See David Gollust, "Clinton Says US Seeking More Help for Anti-Piracy Task Force," *Voice of America* (9 April 2009), http://www.voanews.com/english/2009-04-09-voa61.cfm (accessed 8 May 2009). Admiral Mullen, CJCS, and Vice Admiral William Gortney, the top naval officer charged with responsibility for battling piracy, have repeatedly emphasized the futility of a maritime struggle with pirates. See Tom Bowman, "Pentagon Looks Beyond Force to Counter Piracy," National Public Radio (5 May 2009), http://www.npr.org/templates/story/story.php?storyId=103790982 (accessed 8 May 2009).

[10] Samuel P. Huntington, *The Soldier and the State: The Theory of Politics and Civil-Military Relations*, 1985 ed. (Cambridge, MA: The Belknap Press of Harvard University Press, 1957), 69.

needed instrument of national power.[11] With regard to piracy, US military inaction sent a clear signal of isolationist intent. Even after a VLCC, critical in the smooth transportation of the world's most critical energy commodity, had been successfully hijacked, the US posture on piracy remained one of insignificant involvement coupled with mere rhetoric encouraging multilateral action. It seems that neither the *Sirius Star* nor the *Faina* had a sufficiently chilling effect on the collective US military security consciousness to disrupt isolationist desires with respect to piracy.

Nor did the spokespersons for US economic interests champion increased military involvement. The economic effect of Somali piracy on US interests did not change a great deal in 2008. Even though the year did see large ransoms paid and valuable ships seized, the effects observed on the shipping industry as a whole were minimal and easily absorbed by the private insurance system. Aside from some notable and daring counter-attacks by French and US forces, the tried and true way to deal with Somali pirates was and is to engage in negotiation for the ship's and crew's safe return. Protest about piracy remained mostly in the shipping trade press; businesses did not give voice to it in the light of more pressing economic concerns. In sum, historic national trends, IR elite rhetoric, military conservatism, and the relatively low economic impact of piracy all shaped an isolationist cultural preference with respect to the problem of piracy.

Secondary Response: "Forced" Interventionism

In spite of these multiple reasons for US security elites to continue an isolationist response to the specific issue of Somali piracy, the interest of rivals, especially Russia and China, in the problem appears to have forced a hurried response to Somali piracy. An expert observer of the US Navy's response concluded that CTF-151's stand-up occurred rapidly and in response to "non-friendly countries" sending ships to the area, even though proximate cause for additional involvement existed for months or years prior.[12] At that time, US patience with multilateral response and willingness to stand aside and encourage other nations to provide that response gave way to a pressing national security concern demanding immediate unilateral involvement. The brief capture of an American-flagged ship and an extended hostage ordeal with its captain

---

[11] Eliot A. Cohen, *Supreme Command: Soldiers, Statesmen, and Leadership in Wartime*, 2003 ed. (New York: Anchor Books, 2002), 118.
[12] Linardi, 2009 discussion.

further galvanized the political response that rival foreign involvement started. After the *Maersk Alabama* incident, Secretary of State Clinton's rhetoric against pirates became bolder, including criticism of NATO countries who release captured pirates.[13] Figure 7 represents IR elites' appreciation of the emerging constraints within the framework described in chapter 3.

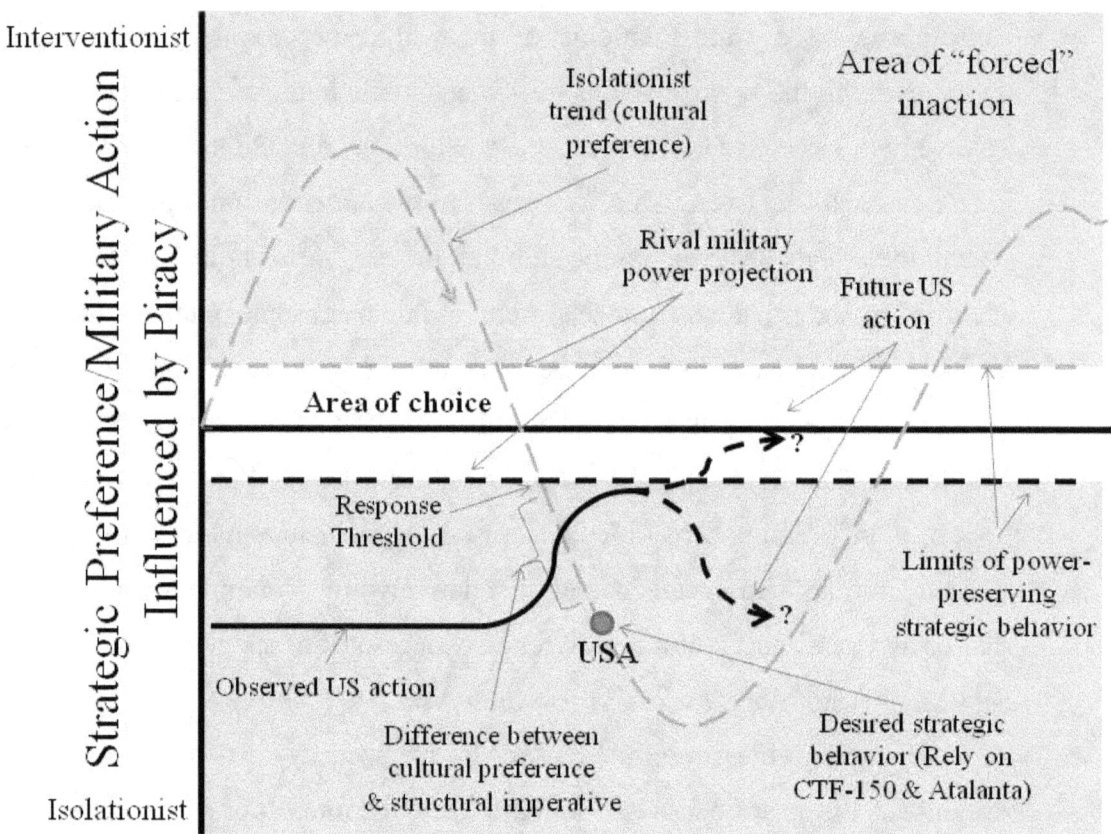

Figure 7: Structural limits, cultural preference, & US military response to Somali piracy
Source: Author's original work

In the case of Somali piracy, US IR elites had coalesced into an isolationist area of the military response spectrum (the point labeled "USA"). Absent other forces, these elites have the power to control US military involvement so that it conforms to their desires. As noted in chapter 3, isolationist elites have a higher probability of success in seeing actual national behavior conform to their desires, because isolationism is a dominant American strategic cultural bias. For piracy, the cultural preference caused

---

[13] "Somalia: Clinton Criticizes the Release of Somali Pirates," *The New York Times*, 20 April 2009, A8.

policy to stagnate in an isolationist gray area; the military involvement the United States pursued was too timid when measured against the structural expectations imposed on the world's leading superpower. External military actions of rival nations, however, had a limiting effect on the influence of strategic culture elites, and US policy moved closer to an area of minimum structural requirements (the white area in figure 7).

The Russian and Chinese decisions to send anti-piracy fleets to the Gulf of Aden and other areas affected by Somali pirates comprised the main structural constraints on US military action. The well-publicized capture of an innocent American citizen imposed additional political constraints, and these served to reinforce the response driven by Russian and Chinese involvement. The horizontal dashed lines represent these constraints. The solid black line representing US military response moves in reaction to these constraints. With a significant projection of rival military power into this area, observed US behavior took a tack at odds with previous rhetoric, behavior, and the expressed wishes of strategic cultural elites. The change in behavior implies that the Russian and Chinese action crossed a response threshold (in this case, the lower dashed horizontal line), a point at which a nation's options must accommodate the actions of other actors rather than its own internal preferences. Specifically, the Russian and Chinese actions set a response standard that the US must not only meet, but exceed, if it is to fulfill its role as the sole leading superpower with respect to piracy—or any other matter.

The line representing US behavior rises to meet the structural constraints, but the line for future behavior shows two possible, divergent paths. As mentioned above, the current US enthusiasm for US intervention may be a short-lived political outcome of the *Maersk Alabama* incident rather than a long-term calculated response. Thus, this argument considers two possibilities for future behavior. In the first, US military response stays at a level beyond other powers striving in the area. It leads an effort against piracy, effectively controlling it. In the second scenario, US behavior falls off again to match its prevailing elites' strategic cultural preferences. In accordance with the discussion in chapter 3, an enduring mismatch between cultural preference and structural constraints can prevent national behavior from responding adequately to the structural constraints. The result is a loss of national power.

Arguing that IR elites' chosen strategic culture preference is moot in the face of other nation's actions puts the theory of strategic culture at odds with that of structural realism. The individuals able to influence strategic culture are usually those in power within a given administration. Somali piracy is not an existential threat to the United States, and its economic impact is not great, so continued inaction would not immediately threaten the current elite's hold on power, and continued isolationism seems to remain a viable response. A proposed mechanism for resolving this apparent conflict is a central proposition of this investigation. In other words, this thesis offers an explanation as to why good foreign policy decisions must accommodate both strategic cultural preference and structural realist demands at the same time.

This thesis proposes that the frameworks of strategic culture and structural realism combine with the effect of explaining one another. Chapter 3 identified three distinct schools: (1) strategic culturalists who believe that national behavior is malleable in the hands of elites, (2) strategic culturalists who believe that national behavior is more enduring in character, but still shaped by internal national choice, and (3) structuralists who view national behavior as ineluctable responses to other actors. Within the proposed mechanism, all three schools contribute to understanding real-world national behavior. The mechanism is easiest to understand in an ordered sequence.

First, the short-term nature of strategic culture offered by the first school is in view through national policy directives and security rhetoric. Influential national security elites gaining power in 2008 made it clear that their desired posture for overall US military involvement was more isolationist than that of the previous administration. The initial military response to Somali piracy anticipated and reflected these desires. Next, the ideas of the third school come into view with the recognition that other nations have the ability to impose a strategic response threshold on the internal desires of national security elites. Russian and Chinese involvement in anti-piracy actions constituted a bright-line event to which a US response was almost mandatory, in spite of prevailing cultural desires. Standing up CTF-151 as a demonstration of unilateral commitment is an example of the effects structural forces can have.[14]

Finally, the model relies on the perspective of the second school to resolve the conflict between culture and structure, providing closure on what really drives national behavior. The second school consists of culturalists who acknowledge that there is an enduring quality to a nation's strategic culture—they may tie it to an unchangeable quality like geography, but assert that it is not as malleable in the hands of elites as the first school argues. This thesis offers that what is truly enduring about strategic culture are those things to which a nation thinks it must respond. In other words, its strategic culture reflects the way it sees itself within a structural realist construct. In the case of Somali piracy, the United States saw that it must respond to rival military power projections in international sea-lanes. This mandatory, "structured" response is really a manifestation of strategic culture.

If structured perceptions and responses are at their roots cultural, they are in fact subject to preference and choice, which counters structural realism at a fundamental level. Realizing this, the thesis does not go so far as to argue that structural constraints always win out. It is possible for a nation to respond to stimuli in a manner inconsistent with its current role in the global power structure. The cause of this may be external or internal. External causes might be a proximate loss of power: an empire loses colonies to revolution or a country experiences a significant military disaster. The internal causes relate to national will: a nation abdicates fulfilling its role in world affairs. This thesis identifies a hesitancy of the United States to fulfill its superpower role with regard to piracy. Chapter 3 asserted that a possible outcome of this course of action would be a loss of national power; the paragraphs below explain how that loss of power might occur.

In an argument detailing a strategy of *selective engagement*, Robert Art lists "preventing…destructive security competitions among the Eurasian great powers" and

---

[14] CTF-151's establishment is an elegant example of unilateral commitment garnished by international cooperation. CTF-151 was a US Navy-led task force when it stood up. It had a US commander and a nucleus of US ships, albeit with a standing invitation to other nations to join. After establishing a new level of commitment to piracy efforts through CTF-151, the US Navy immediately began to advertise the task force's multilateral *bona fides*. See "Somalia: Turkish-Led CTF-151 Makes First Suspected Pirate Capture," *AllAfrica.com* (18 May 2009), http://allafrica.com/stories/200905180555.html (accessed 20 May 2009).

"preserving an open international economic order" among six critical US interests.[15] He proceeds to advocate selective engagement, which emphasizes US leadership in the context of realist ideology, but eschews both haphazard military action and unilateral action. Art's ideal of selective engagement is appropriate for piracy, but the outcomes of failing to engage at the right times are pertinent to the present discussion. A lack of US leadership early in the pirate crisis caused both competition among Eurasian world powers (European, Russian, and Chinese navies all sailing in close proximity) and destruction of an open economic order (the chilling effect of piracy on global shipping).

Art offers isolationism as an undesirable alternative to selective engagement.[16] In addition to undermining the national interests of Eurasian harmony and economic order, isolationism ignores useful US alliances, makes future military action more difficult, and fails to hedge against future risk.[17] Thus a failure to lead when structural constraints demand it, though possible, is inadvisable, because it serves to undermine vital US interests over the long term. Considering arguments for and against US military involvement in other recent conflicts underscores the application of this model.

Fred Kaplan, along with many others, has argued that strategic cultural preferences of national security elites in President George W. Bush's administration pushed the United States into an undesirable war with Iraq in 2003. Kaplan argues that indulging the cultural preference for intervention in the face of more isolationist structural constraints ultimately diminished US power, making "America less fearsome."[18] Adding Kaplan's criticism of US foreign policy to the model used here to describe the response to piracy might yield a depiction like the one in figure 8.

[15] Robert J. Art, "The Strategy of Selective Engagement," in *The Use of Force: Military Power and International Politics*, ed. Robert J. Art and Kenneth N. Waltz (Lanham, MD: Rowman and Littlefield Publishers, Inc., 2004), 300.

[16] Art, "The Strategy of Selective Engagement," 317.

[17] Art, "The Strategy of Selective Engagement," 317–18.

[18] Fred Kaplan, *Daydream Believers: How a Few Grand Ideas Wrecked American Power* (Hoboken, NJ: John Wiley and Sons, Inc., 2008), 199.

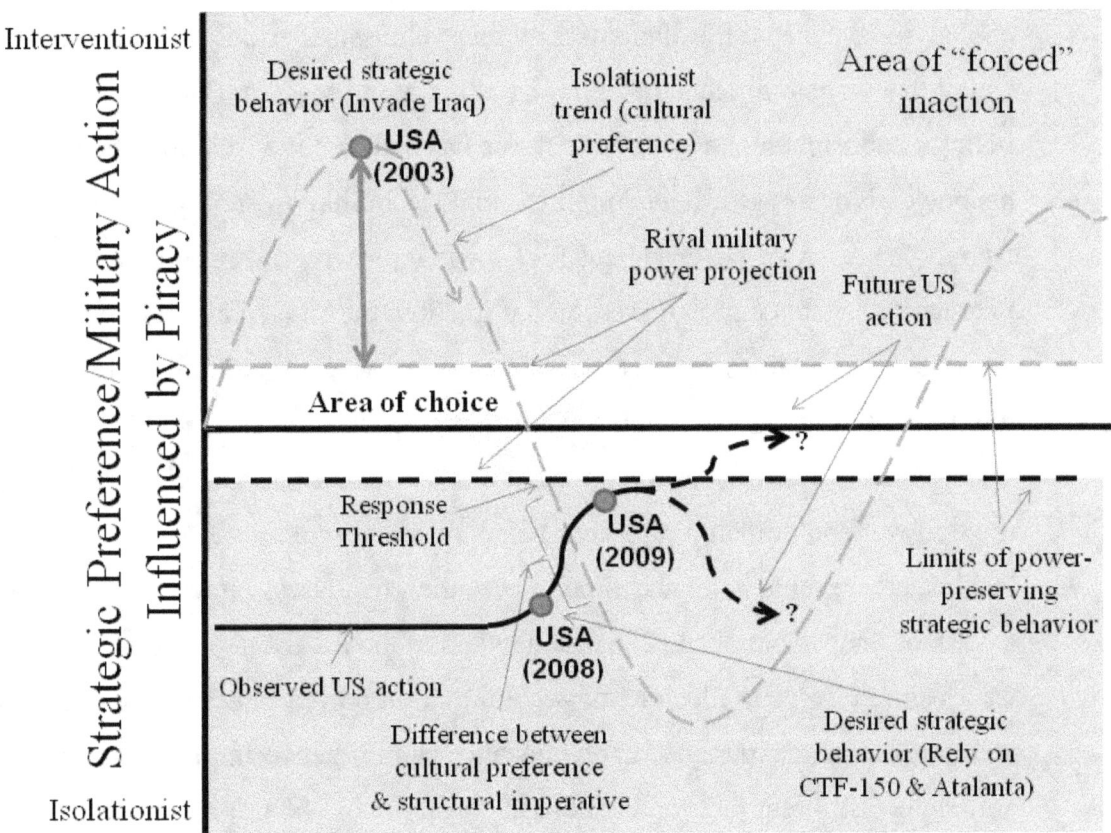

Figure 8: Structural limits & cultural preferences, 2003 Iraq War
Source: Author's original work

According to Kaplan's analysis, the strategic cultural preference of national security elites for intervention in Iraq drove a US invasion of Iraq that went significantly beyond the United States' role in world affairs. Since the preferences of elites never did become reconciled with the structural imperatives, Kaplan argues, the United States never "fac[ed] up to the limits of America's power." Kaplan acknowledges that "America is the only nation theoretically capable of global leadership" because of its economic, military, and political might. In his view, though, a mismatch between cultural preference and structural constraint (represented in the model by a double-ended arrow in figure 8) "undermined America's authority as a legal or moral arbiter."[19]

This thesis does not judge the motivation for or the effect on US power brought about by the 2003 invasion of Iraq. Kaplan's views serve only to represent how a model

---

[19] Kaplan, *Daydream Believers*, 195–97.

that combines notions of strategic culture and structural realism are theoretically robust enough to analyze both isolationist and interventionist periods of foreign policy. To the extent that Kaplan reflects the opinions of many in President Barack Obama's foreign policy establishment, however, this thesis has detected the isolationist cultural preference his book advocates as influencing the initial US military response to Somali piracy. If Deputy Secretary of Defense Paul Wolfowitz represented US foreign policy in 2003, and Secretary of State Clinton represented it in 2009, the sinusoidal preference curve in figure 8 offers a fair approximation of the rapid swings in cultural preference posited by the first of the strategic cultural schools described in chapter 3.

Such caricatures of foreign policy are of course simplistic. In reality, the issue of the Iraq war and Somali piracy are of such different scales as to frustrate comparison. For instance, even a large maritime intervention to address piracy would require less than a tenth of the personnel and expense devoted to the invasion of Iraq.[20] The two separate issues simply serve to illustrate how cultural preferences can fluctuate over time, and how a culture-shaping experience in one instance can influence another scenario with completely different facts and structural constraints. The last portion of this thesis draws out lessons at three levels of policy that follow from a consideration of the dynamic tension between cultural preference and structural constraints.

Lessons from Piracy

Discussions of military force often divide its application into three separate levels: strategic, operational, and tactical. The strategic level considers matters of national policy. At this level, national interests most clearly shape the use of military force. The strategic level shows in sharp relief Clausewitz's dictum that "war is not merely an act of policy but a true political instrument, a continuation of political intercourse, carried on with other means."[21] The operational level links strategy to tactics. It coordinates battlefield actions on a large scale while keeping the political ends and constraints in mind. The operational level of war is the domain of generals. Again, Clausewitz offers a

---

[20] This is true only for a substantial *maritime* effort. An invasion of Somalia, based on the land area in question and the degree of internal anarchy, would be as big or bigger than the Iraq war effort. Even though the instances may differ in the scope of the military footprint required to prosecute them, the analogy of cyclic preferences in IR still holds. How many chances for small instances of intervention did the United States forego in the aftermath of Vietnam, for example?

[21] Carl von Clausewitz, *On War*, ed. Michael Eliot Howard and Peter Paret, trans. Michael Eliot Howard and Peter Paret, Revised ed. (Princeton, NJ: Princeton University Press, 1984), 87.

helpful summary: "When all is said and done, it really is the commander's *coup d'oeil*, his ability to see things simply, to identify the whole business of war completely with himself, that is the essence of good generalship."[22] Certainly, Clausewitz refers to the general's ability to see both the larger strategic political constraints around him as well as battlefield opportunities and challenges. The tactical level encompasses the use of force. For battles between similar opposing forces in a context of unlimited war, it is at the tactical level that warfare most closely approximates Clausewitz's abstraction that says "[w]ar is nothing but a duel on a larger scale."[23] Since unlimited wars between evenly matched forces are historically rare, tactical realities usually reflect a myriad of nuanced constraints that flow down from the larger political goals driving the use of force.

Strategic Lessons

Somali piracy offers lessons for strategic decision makers. Because IR elites comprise the true strategic decision making body in the United States, they must identify those events that constitute the set of "structural" constraints that underlie a nation's long-term strategic culture. The case of Somali piracy suggests that for the United States, rival nations projecting power in an area of traditional neutrality or US influence is an event requiring an answer. More fundamentally, chapter 2 shows that the responsibility for guaranteeing freedom of passage falls to the dominant superpower. The superpower can attempt to enlist the help of other nations through skillful diplomacy, but can never delegate away the responsibility—dreaming does not bring meaningful results.

Consider Colin Gray's argument that "international order requires a policeman or a policing mechanism." He says further, "Politics are about power…peace is not the product of…formal international institutions." Further, interplay of interests among states does not guarantee order, so "order needs to be organized and kept through positive steps in policy by those with the power to do so."[24] This investigation suggests that this sentiment, coupled with the often-tacit assumption that the United States, or the coalitions it leads, is the *best* policing mechanism when such measures become necessary, approaches a deeper understanding of US "deep" strategic culture. This interpretation

---

[22] Clausewitz, *On War*, 578.
[23] Clausewitz, *On War*, 75.
[24] Gray, *Fighting Talk*, 20–21.

supports Art's recommendation to limit Eurasian competition through military leadership, which is exactly what taking a commanding role against Somalia piracy promises to do.

The utility of a dialogue about what truly comprises US deep strategic culture reaches far beyond crafting an appropriate response to Somali piracy. Identifying the type of events that can and should cause an "ineluctable" response from the United States would improve foreign policy decisions. A shared understanding of the nation's baseline by elites from both sides of the isolationist-interventionist ideological spectrum would prevent erratic and emotional responses to IR situations. Besides the projection of military power by rivals identified in this thesis, there are other testable hypotheses for IR actions that require a structural response from a superpower. These include: (1) a new power attempting influence in a geographic area where it had no previous influence; (2) a rival ideology that offers alternatives to democracy and capitalism as dominant political and economic structures; and (3) a competitor's development of asymmetric weapons capabilities for which no adequate defense exists. The first part of this chapter predicted future tension between cultural preference and structural constraints, with a likely outcome of reduced national power if elites are unable to resolve that tension. Anticipating likely conflicts between isolationism and interventionism at the boundary between desired culture and structure may be a way to identify and to prepare in advance for future American military involvement.

Operational Lessons

The main lesson from Somali piracy for operational-level decision makers is that the realm of "generalship" extends beyond the military. In an interconnected world of constant communication, *coup d'oeil* must reach well beyond the battlefield. Because of the character of warfare in Clausewitz's day, this statement in his era would have seemed puzzling. In the eighteenth century, distance separated a general from political influence for discrete periods—months or years might pass in the prosecution of a distant military campaign. Today's world does not allow for such separation, and the commander must always have the political ends in mind; reporting to the sovereign for an update every few weeks cannot adequately keep pace with political developments. Since the complexity of war has grown since the eighteenth century, however, the only way to effect such constant consideration of the political side of war is to create functioning dialogue between operational military commanders and their counterparts in diplomatic organizations.

Consider an apparent lack of this kind of communication in the case of Somali piracy as an illustration. In late February 2009, US Deputy Assistant Secretary of Defense David Sedney used the nexus of anti-piracy operations as a springboard for optimism about future US-Chinese military relations, even though there is no cooperation beyond simply preventing collision of the warships. Chinese Major General Qian Lihua gave a more adequate reflection of the true status of military relations, giving a stoic demand for "the US side to take concrete measures for the resumption and development of our military ties."[25] Sedney's statements reflected the surface-level desires of his government's elites; the behavior he mischaracterized was a reflection of structural requirements and hence a deeper strategic culture. His words were anachronistic, not because they lagged the circumstances, but because the circumstances do not align with prevailing rhetoric.[26]

Sedney's words may or may not have truly reflected a lack of understanding of the competitive nature of the US and Chinese naval operations to combat Somali piracy—the language of diplomacy allows for both hyperbole and understatement. The larger point is that communication must span a wide range of executive departments at the operational level to integrate military capability with political ends. Allowing that Sedney made a deliberate mischaracterization of Chinese "cooperation" in the Gulf of Aden as a diplomatic gesture to China, would his counterparts in the State Department realize the subtlety? After the press conference where he made those remarks, did Sedney explain to the CTF-151 commander his ostensible appreciation for the true nature of US and Chinese operations? Would CTF-151 have been listening?

Acknowledging the difficulty of lateral communication, the US Air Force's official doctrine on irregular warfare states, "Unity of effort across all instruments of

---

[25] Christopher Bodeen, "US Praises China Anti-Piracy Role Off Somalia," *Associated Press* (2009), http://www.google.com/hostednews/ap/article/ALeqM5jzzULJt2ZiW2IZR3KKuViEpbOAlQD96KHO980 (accessed 4 March 2009).
[26] This is a surface-level interpretation of Sedney's words. It is likely, given his more than 25 years of involvement with Chinese affairs that he appreciated the true character of the operation.

power is essential to overall strategic success."[27] Given that elites do not communicate well enough to agree on true strategic imperatives, this unity is elusive at best. At the operational level, diplomatic and military implementers of strategy characteristically have even fewer opportunities to engage in dialogue. It is critical that operational diplomats and generals seek lateral communication of their own volition to achieve the goals the nation asks of them. Effective operational commanders will realize that even though they cannot survey the entirety of modern day theatres of war as Napoleon could, "seasoned judgment and an instinct born of long experience" are no less necessary in today's world.[28] Further, commanders can only hope to achieve this judgment if they rely on the expertise of others, who bring the same level of responsibility and knowledge to bear with a different area of expertise. As the battlefield has grown too big for one mind to take it all in at a glance, so also have IR problem sets grown too big for a single individual's mental capability.

An example of this cross-specialty collaboration from Somali piracy is US influence on international law. The US armed forces, the US legal system, and US diplomatic organizations have all made contributions in the legal battle against piracy. The legal status of pirates and international law about their prosecution are core themes of this thesis. While some apparent confusion about these legal matters is really a political delay tactic, reputable publications still bemoan lack of legal clarity with apparent sincerity.[29] Diplomatic statements, domestic judicial proceedings, and military attorneys can help in this regard. The opinions they offer about pirate prosecution will define the worldwide state of the art. Since global popular opinion and political will against pirates align in strength, decisive opinions from US legal bodies can shape flexible legal options for combating piracy for the next several decades.

A series of US actions in May 2009 demonstrated to the world US leadership in both military and legal prosecution of piracy. First, the US Navy, cooperating with South Korean naval forces, boarded and captured 17 piracy suspects on a mothership.[30] The US

---

[27] T. Michael Mosely, "Doctrine Document 2–3, Irregular Warfare," ed. Department of the Air Force (1 August 2007), 8.

[28] Clausewitz, *On War*, 517.

[29] "Wrong Signals," *The Economist*, 7 May 2009.

[30] "US Navy Detains 17 on Suspected Pirate 'Mothership'," *Associated Press* (14 May 2009), http://www.foxnews.com/story/0,2933,520153,00.html (accessed 25 May 2009).

Navy announced that Kenya would serve as the prosecution venue for these suspects, an announcement that preceded French and Spanish declarations about turning over recently captured piracy suspects to Kenyan authorities.[31] Just a day prior, a US State Department press release highlighted US diplomatic leadership with regard to piracy.[32] In a matter of months, coordinated US action in various executive departments at an operational level has defined an international norm for prosecuting pirates, which has emboldened the efforts of all nations tackling the problem.

Tactical Lessons

The lessons derived thus far share a theme of looking beyond one's sphere of comfort to improve IR decisions. Elites must look beyond their cultural preferences to identify the foundations of US interests. Operational decision makers must look beyond their areas of expertise, engaging their counterparts across government to achieve a level of knowledge that is a match for the wicked problems facing the United States. The same is true for those who would implement strategy at the tactical level. In this case, looking outside the sphere of comfort involves anticipating likely IR trends and having practical ways to implement them when strategic and operational decision makers decide upon a course of action.

In the case of Somali piracy, the US Navy at a tactical level has made an admirable response to piracy. The effort reflected in standing up CTF-151 is an appropriate action. This response was clearly US-led, focused on the specific problem of piracy without having to accommodate other mission sets, and allowed for the incorporation of other international assets in due course. The approach played to all of the United States' strengths, and still accommodated the prevailing cultural preference for international cooperation. It is worth saying here that an invasion of Somalia to root out pirate camps as part of a larger attempt to install a stable Somali regime is *not* appropriate now: this goes well beyond the level of the structural challenge put forward by US rivals. Piracy today is not the same existential threat that drove Pompey's no-holds-barred approach in ancient Rome. Even though UN resolutions allow an invasion of Somalia to

---

[31] "French Hand over 11 Suspected Pirates to Kenya." See also "Spain Hands over Suspected Somali Pirates to Kenya," *Agence France-Presse* (16 May 2009), http://www.google.com/hostednews/afp/article/ ALeqM5h6s_KO1Cq6OulA9uEBH26vVXUD4A (accessed 25 May 2009).
[32] "Taking Diplomatic Action against Piracy," ed. Bureau of Public Affairs (US Department of State, 13 May 2009).

combat piracy, the cultural preference for isolationism on that front is appropriate. Such a degree of interventionism would result in US military overstretch.[33]

Though the maritime military response to piracy was appropriate, the US military could have done even more to anticipate and communicate the structural challenge of piracy through tactical actions. To wit, the military effort should have involved greater incorporation of air power. In its current incarnation, the anti-piracy effort is already airpower-intensive. Rotary-winged aircraft act as the long-range eyes of all anti-piracy fleets, providing the ability to search roughly a 100 nautical mile radius around a naval vessel. Helicopters also provide the force to deter pirates, carrying armed sailors of all nationalities to points of confrontation with pirate ships. With regard to fixed-wing assets, US Navy P-3 Orions perform extended-range search duty of the kind integral to locating and tracking the *Maersk Alabama*.[34]

To counter piracy in wide expanses of open seas, media commentators have pointed out the invaluable contributions of fixed-wing aircraft performing increased search functions.[35] The most intractable part of the piracy problem is the huge area in need of patrol. Fixed-wing aircraft can immediately locate suspect ships and extend radio range so that merchants under attack have a chance of summoning help before pirates can mount a successful attack.[36] From the US Air Force perspective, a failure to engage in the anti-piracy mission is unfortunate on two fronts. First, the USAF has aircraft ideally suited to perform wide area maritime search, including the E-3 Sentry airborne warning and control system. Engagements in Iraq and Afghanistan have limited availability of these platforms in the Gulf of Aden and Indian Ocean so far, but their utility is unmistakable.

The second reason the US Air Force should seek involvement in the anti-piracy mission is a symbolic gesture. If the United States embraces the anti-piracy mission as this thesis argues it should, a joint effort by its two military services best equipped to undertake that mission signals serious commitment to the world. There is a tendency for

---

[33] US military involvement inside Somalia last occurred in 2003, when 18 US soldiers died in operations against a Somali warlord in Mogadishu.

[34] Howard Pankratz, "Two Coloradans Played Role in US Skipper's Pirate Rescue," *The Denver Post* (5 May 2009), http://www.denverpost.com/news/ci_12300500 (accessed 8 May 2009).

[35] Jonathan Saul, "Planes Seen as Crucial against Somali Piracy," *Reuters* (28 April 2009), http://www.reuters.com/article/worldNews/idUSTRE53R4LX20090428 (accessed 8 May 2009).

[36] Linardi, .

the US Navy to hold exclusive domain over maritime aerial reconnaissance operations, even when the US Air Force could make a valid contribution. The contentious March 1948 Key West Conference, which outlined roles and missions for the armed services after WWII, identified maritime search as the domain of the US Navy. Because the main argument at Key West was the role of naval air power in the context of the US nuclear arsenal, the air service tacitly conceded the right of the naval service to have exclusive purview of maritime reconnaissance.[37] Exclusion of the Air Force from such missions has been systemic, with neither service challenging this conventional wisdom.[38] This artificial limitation could have deleterious effects for the US military in a larger war, though. It is ironic that smaller air forces in possession of the same kinds of platforms do not limit their use in maritime operations, and the air forces of Canada and Australia, among others, have contributed to anti-piracy maritime operations when the US Air Force has not.[39] It is precisely because US military forces each have enough air power to hold exclusive sway over certain mission sets that joint prosecution of piracy would send such a clear message: it signals that national policy is strong enough to overcome significant bureaucratic inertia.

In addition to specific lessons that piracy suggests, recognizing the general possibility for tension between cultural preference and structural imperatives can also equip people serving national interests at a tactical level. A responsible tactician will recognize the confluence of cultural and structural forces that influence her ability to act. One should avoid quixotic battlefield stands against electoral and bureaucratic inertia. Even if muddled strategy contributes to tactical ineffectiveness, idealistic stands too far out of alignment with current trends skirt the line of insubordination if they do not blatantly cross it. At the same time, the tactician must not allow cultural inertia to swing

---

[37] Jeffrey G. Barlow, *Revolt of the Admirals: The Fight for Naval Aviation 1945–1950* (Washington, DC: Government Reprints Press, 2001), 123, 325.

[38] This is not to assign "blame" to the US Navy for the US Air Force's lack of maritime reconnaissance work, as reluctance for these missions dates back to the US Army Air Corps. A 1943 report detailing successful ocean reconnaissance missions from the Seventh Fighter Wing has a dismissive scrawl from an unidentified higher headquarters: "not advisable as an AAF mission." The comment is in the margin and appears next to two circled words: "sea sweeps." See C.H. Ridenour, "Methods of Bombing Shipping Targets," (Headquarters Seventh Fighter Wing, 20 February 1943).

[39] Kevin Ferdinand, (Major, Royal Canadian Air Force), in discussion with the author, 6 November 2008. See also "Australian Forces to Battle Somalian [*sic*] Pirates," *The Australian* (29 May 2009), http://www.theaustralian.news.com.au/story/0,25197,25555122-12377,00.html (accessed 31 May 2009).

so far that it impairs or destroys military readiness. A tactician committed to a greater cause than the present battle will expend personal effort to keep alive military options out of favor with current national preferences. Hair-trigger interventionism and isolationist unpreparedness are equally undesirable.[40] Tacticians, the guardians of military skill sets, can keep some valuable capabilities from reaching the ash heap of discarded military capacity. It is useful to remember that the historic US tendency is toward isolationism— at least this is how most historians describe the US tendency in IR.[41] In an era of relative calm or post-war drawdown, the most difficult task of a tactical leader is to prevent excessive truncation of military skills. Most often, that tactician will achieve this goal by moving on to the operational and perhaps strategic levels—political influence is scarce at the tactical level of any organization.

Conclusion

This thesis has offered a history of piracy around the world, demonstrating that the task of fighting pirates belongs to hegemons and superpowers. Serious bouts of piracy in history indicate a lack of strong international leadership that fosters global peace and prosperity. The thesis has described Somali piracy, demonstrating that its growth in the first decade of the twenty-first century represents a serious security challenge worthy of superpower response. It offers a theoretical comparison of strategic culture and structural realism, demonstrating the possibility for and ramifications of differences between national strategic preference and international structural imperatives. Finally, the thesis applies this historical perspective and theoretical treatment to the US response to Somali piracy.

Here is the crux of the matter: it is true that elite opinions coalesce in such a way as to influence the preferred posture for use of military force. Recently, the US strategic preference has become isolationist in this regard. It is also true that there are thresholds of lawlessness or adversarial action that outweigh these desired postures. Nations,

---

[40] In Art's words, "selective engagement is wary of the risks of military entanglement overseas, but unlike isolationism, it believes that some entanglements either lower the chances of war or are necessary to protect important American interests even at the risk of war." See Art, "The Strategy of Selective Engagement," 318.

[41] Some historians, of course, take a different view. Fred Anderson and Andrew Cayton argue that "American wars have either expressed a certain kind of imperial ambition or have resulted directly from successes in previous imperial conflicts." See Fred Anderson and Andrew Cayton, *The Dominion of War: Empire and Liberty in North America 1500–2000* (New York: Penguin Group, 2005), xiv.

especially superpowers like the United States, who ignore these thresholds to maintain a cultural *status quo,* do so at the risk of stability and prosperity in the world system they lead. Observed US actions that fly in the face of elite opinion—a superpower "just doing what it has to do"—can send a signal that the underlying strategic culture is robust and in tune with structural realities. In the case of Somali piracy, renewed US leadership to remove the scourge of the seas portends that the nation is willing to maintain its superpower mantle. Failing to do so will only encourage continued piracy, and it will send the message that the world's leading superpower does not put the highest value on rule of law or an open international economic order.

Piracy is a contemporary example with which to illustrate the disparity potential between strategic culture and structural imperatives. Because of piracy's historical role in establishing and signaling the demise of superpowers, it remains cogent today. Not every international problem is as significant as piracy, but several carry the same level of *gravitas.* Examples of this kind of issue include the spread of weapons of mass destruction, genocide, and unchecked aggression by one country against another. The contradictory responses of the US military to piracy off the east African coast constitute a strategic conundrum, but the nation will solve the puzzle with success if it continues to act in the leadership role it adopted in 2009. Piracy is a strategic threshold—a time when structural imperatives outweigh cultural preferences. National decision makers will do well to remember that concept when other weighty problems of statecraft arise. As Waltz argued, "If the leading power does not lead, the others cannot follow."[42] The United States has started to lead the battle against Somali piracy. It should continue to lead with confidence.

---

[42] Waltz, *Theory of International Politics,* 210.

Bibliography

Academic Papers

Cobb, Christopher B.R. "Combatting Maritime Piracy." Master's Degree Thesis, Naval Postgraduate School, 1994.

Articles (no author listed)

"African, Middle East States Seek Legal Reforms to Try Pirates." *EasyBourse* (26 January 2009), http://www.easybourse.com/bourse-actualite/marches/african-middle-east-states-seek-legal-reforms-to-try-603591 (accessed 26 January 2009).

"Ahoy There." *The Economist*, 22 November 2008.

"Armed Response." *Lloyd's List*, 30 October 2008, 7.

"Australian Forces to Battle Somalian [*sic*] Pirates." *The Australian* (29 May 2009), http://www.theaustralian.news.com.au/story/0,25197,25555122-12377,00.html (accessed 31 May 2009).

"Body of a Somali Pirate, Carrying $153,000 of a Ransom, Washes Ashore." *The New York Times*, 12 January 2009, A7.

"Boxer Becomes Piracy Task Force Flagship." *Navy Times* (10 March 2009), http://www.navytimes.com/news/2009/03/navy_flagship151_031009/ (accessed 11 March 2009).

"Briefing: Africa's Prospects--Opportunity Knocks." *The Economist*, 11 October 2008.

"China Begins Somalia Piracy Patrols." *Aljazeera.net* (7 January 2009), http://english.aljazeera.net/news/asia-pacific/2009/01/20091752314617900.html (accessed 7 January 2009).

"China to Renew Somalia Anti-Piracy Mission." *Associated Press* (8 March 2009), http://www.google.com/hostednews/ap/article/ALeqM5i0A_UOu6oEtFNUxbNB FFThfSfCwgD96QCSGO0 (accessed 9 March 2009).

"Dutch Courts to Try Pirates Now Held in Denmark." *The International Herald Tribune* (15 January 2009), http://www.iht.com/articles/ap/2009/01/15/europe/EU-Netherlands-Pirates.php (accessed 16 January 2009).

"European Parliament Moves to Redefine Piracy as Criminal Act." *Lloyd's List*, 30 October 2008, 2.

"Factbox: Ships Held by Somali Pirates." *Reuters* (2 April 2009), http://www.reuters.com/article/africaCrisis/idUSL2564857 (accessed 3 April 2009).

"French Hand over 11 Suspected Pirates to Kenya." *Associated Press* (8 May 2009), http://www.google.com/hostednews/ap/article/

ALeqM5gB7YMEDuCwwY9ncDOtPAkEI4-H2wD9824F680 (accessed 24 May 2009).

"French Navy Foils Somali Pirate Attack." *AFP* (27 January 2009), http://www.google.com/hostednews/afp/article/ALeqM5iniI4Hpem2JKcN1RtzJU5KGA9pWw (accessed 28 January 2009).

"French Troops Kill Somali Pirate to Free Hostages." *Birmingham Post*, 17 September 2008, 9.

"Indonesia, Malaysia, Singapore Launch Coordinated Patrol of Malacca Strait." *The Jakarta Post* (20 July 2004), http://yaleglobal.yale.edu/display.article?id=4271 (accessed 11 February 2009).

"Iraq Declared New Piracy Hotspot." *International Chamber of Commerce* (31 January 2006), http://www.iccwbo.org/iccfgbd/index.html (accessed 3 April 2009).

"NATO Unveils Maritime Security Mission." *Lloyd's List*, 27 October 2008, 1.

"Naval Forces Establish Somalia Safety Zone." *Lloyd's List*, 26 August 2008, 1.

"Naval Patrols Hampering Somali Pirates: EU, NATO." *Agence France-Presse* (13 May 2009), http://www.google.com/hostednews/afp/article/ALeqM5iUS4J797xQlTxtQ21pR0qTJXUztg (accessed 14 May 2009).

"Opt-out Puts Navy on Sidelines in Pirate Hunt." *The Copenhagen Post* (15 January 2009), http://www.cphpost.dk/news/latest-news/44368-opt-out-puts-denmark-on-pirate-hunt-sidelines.html (accessed 16 January 2009).

"The Perennial Problem of Overpowering Piracy." *Lloyd's List*, 5 November 2008, 4.

"Piracy and Much Worse." *The Economist*, 4 October 2008, 14–16.

"Pirates Seize British Cargo Ship in Gulf of Aden." *CNN.com* (6 April 2009), http://www.cnn.com/2009/WORLD/africa/04/06/britain.cargo.ship.seized.somalia/ (accessed 7 April 2009).

"Privateers." (17 July 2006), http://www.globalsecurity.org/military/agency/navy/privateer.htm (accessed 31 March 2009).

"A Real Network of Terror?" *The Economist*, 11 September 2008.

"Russian Warship on Somali Pirate Mission to Enter Gulf of Aden." *BBC Worldwide Monitoring*, 26 October 2008, 1.

"Somali Pirates Extradited to Netherlands." *Voice of America* (10 February 2009), http://www.voanews.com/english/2009-02-10-voa43.cfm (accessed 11 February 2009).

"Somali Pirates on Hijacking Spree." *Agence France-Presse* (3 April 2009), http://www.google.com/hostednews/afp/article/ALeqM5i_VnXVh5B4FqQzfBeQX-UuQC-tkw (accessed 7 April 2009).

"Somali Pirates Seize Cargo Ship, 20 US Sailors." *MSNBC.com* (8 April 2009), http://www.msnbc.msn.com/id/30103371/ (accessed 8 April 2009).

"Somali Pirates Seize German Ship." *BBC News* (29 January 2009), http://news.bbc.co.uk/1/hi/world/africa/7858462.stm (accessed 30 January 2009).

"Somalia: Inside a Pirate Network." *Integrated Regional Information Networks* (13 January 2009), http://www.irinnews.org/Report.aspx?ReportId=82339 (accessed 13 January 2009).

"Somalia: Turkish-Led CTF-151 Makes First Suspected Pirate Capture." *AllAfrica.com* (18 May 2009), http://allafrica.com/stories/200905180555.html (accessed 20 May 2009).

"Spain Hands over Suspected Somali Pirates to Kenya." *Agence France-Presse* (16 May 2009), http://www.google.com/hostednews/afp/article/ALeqM5h6s_KO1Cq6OulA9uEBH26vVXUD4A (accessed 25 May 2009).

"UN Adopts New Somalia Anti-Piracy Resolution." *Al Arabiya* (8 October 2008), http://www.alarabiya.net/articles/2008/10/08/57866.html (accessed 30 January 2009).

"US Navy Detains 17 on Suspected Pirate 'Mothership'." *Associated Press* (14 May 2009), http://www.foxnews.com/story/0,2933,520153,00.html (accessed 25 May 2009).

"US Navy to Begin Capturing Somali Pirates." *FOCUS News Agency* (16 January 2009), http://www.focus-fen.net/index.php?id=n167345 (accessed 16 January 2009).

"What Congo Means for Obama." *The Economist*, 15 November 2008, 16–17.

"World Piracy Doubles in First Quarter 2009 Due to Somalia." *Reuters* (21 April 2009), http://uk.reuters.com/article/usTopNews/idUKLL13694920090421 (accessed 8 May 2009).

"The World's Most Utterly Failed State." *The Economist*, 4 October 2008, 49–50.

"Wrong Signals." *The Economist*, 7 May 2009.

Articles (author or authors listed)

Anderson, Gary M., and Adam Gifford Jr. "Privateering and the Private Production of Naval Power." *Cato Journal* 11, no. 1 (Spring/Summer 1991): 99–122.

Andersson, Hilary. "China 'Is Fuelling War in Darfur'." (2 October 2008), http://news.bbc.co.uk/2/hi/africa/7503428.stm.

Art, Robert J. "To What Ends Military Power?" *International Security* Vol. 4 (Spring 1980): 4–35.

Beam, Alex. "It Takes a Pillage." *The Boston Globe* (13 January 2009), http://www.boston.com/lifestyle/articles/2009/01/13/it_takes_a_pillage/ (accessed 13 January 2009).

Beckman, Robert C. "Combatting Piracy and Armed Robbery against Ships in Southeast Asia: The Way Forward." *Ocean Development and International Law* 33 (2002): 317–41.

Betts, Richard K. "Is Strategy an Illusion?" *International Security* 25, no. 2 (Fall 2000): 5-50.

Bloomfield, Alan, and Kim Richard Nossal. "Towards an Explicative Understanding of Strategic Culture: The Cases of Australia and Canada." *Contemporary Security Policy* 28, no. 2 (August 2007): 286-307.

Bodeen, Christopher. "US Praises China Anti-Piracy Role Off Somalia." *Associated Press* (3 March 2009), http://www.google.com/hostednews/ap/article/ALeqM5jzzULJt2ZiW2IZR3KKuViEpbOAlQD96KHO980 (accessed 4 March 2009).

Bowman, Tom. "Pentagon Looks Beyond Force to Counter Piracy." *National Public Radio* (5 May 2009), http://www.npr.org/templates/story/story.php?storyId=103790982 (accessed 8 May 2009).

Bryant, Christa Case. "Somali Pirates Free Hijacked Ukrainian Ship." *The Christian Science Monitor* (5 February 2009), http://features.csmonitor.com/globalnews/2009/02/05/somali-pirates-free-hijacked-ukrainian-ship/ (accessed 9 February 2009).

Burgess, Douglas R., Jr. "Piracy Is Terrorism." *The New York Times*, 5 December 2008, A39.

Cherry, Matt, and Amanda Moyer. "US Navy Boards Ship after Pirate Attack." *CNN.com* (7 November 2005), http://www.cnn.com/2005/WORLD/africa/11/07/somalia.pirates/index.html (accessed 2 April 2009).

Childress, Sarah. "Ehtiopia Starts Pullout from Somalia." *The Wall Street Journal*, 14 January 2009, A4.

Chowdhury, Shreya Roy. "Piracy Fallout of Illegal Fishing." *The Times of India* (27 January 2009), http://timesofindia.indiatimes.com/World/Rest_of_World/_Piracy_fallout_of_illegal_fishing/articleshow/4034251.cms (accessed 28 January 2009).

Clenfield, Jason. "Japan to Consider Bill to Fight High-Seas Piracy, Yomiuri Says." *Bloomberg.com* (7 January 2009), http://www.bloomberg.com/apps/news?pid=20601101&sid=a7Uv9IlXyRxw&refer=japan (accessed 7 January 2009).

Cole, August. "Blackwater Plans Effort against Piracy." *The Wall Street Journal*, 3 December 2008, A11.

Costello, Miles. "Somalian Piracy Cripples Shipping with Tenfold Insurance Cost Rises." *The Times*, 11 September 2008, 23.

Crumley, Bruce. "Ridding Somalia of Pirates: Hard Choices for the West." *Time* (29 April 2009), http://www.time.com/time/world/article/0,8599,1894395,00.html (accessed 8 May 2009).

Cummins, Chip. "Pirates Seem Set to Free Saudi Arabian Oil Tanker." *The Wall Street Journal*, 10 January 2009, A4.

Cummins, Chip, Louise Radnofsky, and Phillip Shishkin. "US Ship Repels Pirates." *The Wall Street Journal*, 9 April 2009, A1, A10.

Dillon, Dana. "Maritime Piracy: Defining the Problem." *SAIS Review* XXV, no. 1 (Winter-Spring 2005): 155–65.

Dodd, Mark. "RAN Warships to the Rescue as Somali Pirates Flee." *The Australian* (19 May 2009), http://www.theaustralian.news.com.au/story/0,25197,25504378-15084,00.html (accessed 20 May 2009).

Duffield, John S. "Political Culture and State Behavior: Why Germany Confounds Neorealism." *International Organization* 53, no. 4 (Autumn 1999): 771–94.

Edwards, Bonnie. "Maritime Historian Shares Stories of Female Pirates." *Goldsboro (NC) News-Argus* (3 March 2009), http://www.newsargus.com/news/archives/2009/03/03/maritime_historian_shares_stories_of_female_pirates/ (accessed 4 March 2009).

Evangelista, Joe. "Scaling the Tanker Market." *Surveyor* 4, no. 1 (Winter 2002): 5–11.

Evans, Michael. "Island-Consciousness and Australian Strategic Culture." *Institute of Public Affairs Review* 58, no. 2 (July 2006): 21-23.

Ewing, Philip. "Expert: Navy Doesn't Need War on Piracy." *Navy Times* (10 December 2008), http://www.navytimes.com/news/2008/12/navy_pirate_speech_120908w/ (accessed 30 January 2009).

Funk, Patricia, and Peter Kugler. "Identifying Efficient Crime-Combating Policies by VAR Models: The Example of Switzerland." *Contemporary Economic Policy* 21, no. 4 (October 2003): 525–38.

Gersbach, Hans. "The Private and Social Value of Information in Majority Decisions." *Political Behavior* 15 (March 1993): 15–23.

Gettleman, Jeffrey. "Pirates Tell Their Side: They Want Only Money." *The New York Times*, 1 October 2008, A6, A14.

Gettleman, Jeffrey, and Mohammed Ibrahim. "Officials Still Arguing over Leader for Somalia." *The New York Times*, 13 January 2009 2009, A6.

Gollust, David. "Clinton Says US Seeking More Help for Anti-Piracy Task Force." *Voice of America* (9 April 2009), http://www.voanews.com/english/2009-04-09-voa61.cfm (accessed 8 May 2009).

Gordon, Tom. "Birmingham, AL Native Petty Officer Carlos Moore Helps Navy Curb Piracy Off East African Coast." *The Birmingham News* (2 March 2009), http://www.al.com/news/birminghamnews/metro.ssf?/base/news/123598534432480.xml&coll=2 (accessed 4 March 2009).

Gorman, Siobhan, and Sarah Childress. "American Captain Tries to Escape from Sea Pirates." *The Wall Street Journal*, 11 April 2009, A5.

Gray, Colin S. "Out of the Wilderness: Prime Time for Strategic Culture." *Comparative Strategy* 26, no. 1 (2007): 1–20.

Green, Eda. "Borneo: The Land of River and Palm." *Project Canterbury* (1909), http://anglicanhistory.org/asia/sarawak/green/01.html (accessed 2 April 2009).

Groves, Jason. "Navy Won't Arrest These Pirates for Fear They'll Win Asylum to Live Here." *Sunday Express*, 6 November 2008, 38.

Guled, Abdi, and Andrew Cawthorne. "Somali Pirates Say [They] Freed UAE-Owned Cargo Ship." *The Washington Post* (6 May 2009), http://www.washingtonpost.com/wp-dyn/content/article/2009/05/06/AR2009050600976.html (accessed 7 May 2009).

Halloran, Liz. "Obama Wins First Pirate Battle. More to Come." *National Public Radio* (13 April 2009), http://www.npr.org/templates/story/story.php?storyId=103055832 (accessed 14 April 2009).

Hand, Marcus. "Eyes in the Sky See Strait Attacks Slashed to Zero." *Lloyd's List*, 15 April 2008, 1.

Hassan, Abdiquani. "US Navy Hands 9 Pirates to Somali Authorities." *Reuters* (2 March 2009), http://uk.reuters.com/article/africaCrisis/idUKL2660855 (accessed 4 March 2009).

Heath, Michael. "Anti-Piracy Group Meets at UN to Plan Action in Somali Waters." *Bloomberg.com* (15 January 2009), http://www.bloomberg.com/apps/news?pid=20601101&sid=aecphtP0uYZk&refer=japan (accessed 16 January 2009).

Hefling, Kimberly. "Senator Asks Military to Step up Pirate Patrols." *Associated Press* (5 May 2009), http://www.google.com/hostednews/ap/article/ALeqM5jDwPwVBkcirkTon7pMMfS63vhNGgD980AKBO0 (accessed 7 May 2009).

Jentleson, Bruce W. "The Pretty Prudent Public: Post Post-Vietnam American Opinion on the Use of Military Force." *International Studies Quarterly* 36, no. 1 (March 1992): 49–74.

Johnston, Alastair Iain. "Thinking About Strategic Culture." *International Security* 19, no. 4 (Spring 1995): 32–64.

Kaufmann, Chaim D., and Robert A. Pape. "Explaining Costly International Moral Action: Britain's Sixty-Year Campaign against the Atlantic Slave Trade." *International Organization* 53, no. 4 (Autumn 1999): 631-68.

Keyes, Charley. "Clinton 'Deeply Concerned' About Pirate Attacks." *CNN.com* (9 April 2009), http://politicalticker.blogs.cnn.com/2009/04/09/clinton-deeply-concerned-about-pirate-attacks-2/ (accessed 10 April 2009).

Kontorovich, Eugene. "International Legal Responses to Piracy Off the Coast of Somalia." *ASIL Insights* 13, no. 2 (2009).

Landler, Mark. "Appointing Emissaries, Obama and Clinton Stress Diplomacy." *The New York Times*, 22 January 2009, A10.

Langewiesche, William. "Anarchy at Sea." *The Atlantic*, September 2003, 50–80.

Lantis, Jeffrey. "The Moral Imperative of Force: The Evolution of German Strategic Culture in Kosovo." *Comparative Strategy* 21, no. 1 (2002): 21–46.

Lee, Oliver. "The Geopolitics of America's Strategic Culture." *Comparative Strategy* 27, no. 3 (2008): 267–86.

Lord, Carnes. "American Strategic Culture." *Comparative Strategy* 5, no. 3 (1985): 269-93.

Lubold, Gordon. "US Navy Aims to Flex 'Soft Power'." *Christian Science Monitor*, 27 December 2007, 2.

Malan, Douglas S. "Maritime Attorneys Deal with High Seas Piracy." *The Connecticut Law Tribune* (24 April 2009), http://www.law.com/jsp/law/sfb/lawArticleSFB.jsp?id=1202430155573 (accessed 8 May 2009).

Maliti, Tom. "US to Hand over Any Suspected Pirates to Kenya." *Associated Press* (26 January 2009), http://www.google.com/hostednews/ap/article/ALeqM5gB7YMEDuCwwY9ncDOtPAkEI4-H2wD95V0C9G0 (accessed 26 January 2009).

Manski, Charles F. "Search Profiling with Partial Knowledge of Deterrence." *The Economic Journal* 116 (November 2006): F385–F401.

Masoni, Danilo. "Munich Re Sees Piracy Pushing up Marine Premiums." *Reuters* (28 January 2009), http://uk.reuters.com/article/rbssFinancialServicesAndRealEstateNews/idUKLS75104120090128 (accessed 28 January 2009).

Mohamed Omar Hajii. "The Ultimate Solution of Piracy and Extremism." *Somaliland Press* (18 January 2009), http://somalilandpress.com/1172/the-ultimate-solution-of-piracy-and-extremism (accessed 22 January 2009).

Montgomery, David. "Pillage People: Until Their Legacy Becomes a Punch Line, Somali Pirates Sail Scary Cultural Seas." *The Washington Post*, 6 December 2008, C1.

Murphy, Brian. "US Admiral: Pact near for Somali Pirate Trials." *Associated Press* (21 January 2009), http://www.google.com/hostednews/ap/article/ALeqM5gB7YMEDuCwwY9ncDOtPAkEI4-H2wD95SSMOG0 (accessed 22 January 2009).

Nadelmann, Ethan A. "Global Prohibition Regimes: The Evolution of Norms in International Society." *International Organization* 44, no. 4 (Autumn 1990): 479–526.

Norton-Taylor, Richard. "Britain to Lead Fleet of EU Warships to Tackle Pirates." *The Guardian* (19 November 2008), http://www.guardian.co.uk/world/2008/nov/19/piracy-somalia-eu-operation-atalanta (accessed 8 April 2009).

Osler, David. "Fall-Off in Pirate Attacks 'Is Due to Bad Weather'." *Lloyd's List* (23 February 2009), http://www.lloydslist.com/ll/news/fall-off-in-pirate-attacks-is-due-to-bad-weather/1235130291373.htm (accessed 3 April 2009).

———. "Flag of Inconvenience." *Lloyd's List*, 29 August 2008, 9.

Pankratz, Howard. "Two Coloradans Played Role in US Skipper's Pirate Rescue." *The Denver Post* (5 May 2009), http://www.denverpost.com/news/ci_12300500 (accessed 8 May 2009).

Reyes, Brian. "NATO Warships Respond to Piracy Threats Off Africa." *Lloyd's List*, 23 July 2007, 4.

Rittel, Horst W.J., and Melvin M. Webber. "Dilemmas in a General Theory of Planning." *Policy Sciences* 4 (1973): 155-69.

Rivkin, David B., Jr., and Lee A. Casey. "Pirates Exploit Confusion About International Law." *The Wall Street Journal*, 19 November 2008, A21.

Ryu, Alisha. "Nine Countries Sign Agreements to Combat Africa Piracy." *Voice of America* (30 January 2009), http://www.voanews.com/english/2009-01-30-voa33.cfm (accessed 4 February 2009).

———. "Somali Pirates Disrupt Fishing Industry, Increase Fish Stocks." *Voice of America* (26 January 2009), http://www.voanews.com/english/2009-01-26-voa51.cfm.

Sachs, Jeffrey. "Doing the Sums on Africa." *The Economist*, 20 May 2004.

Sakamaki, Sachiko, and Takashi Hirokawa. "Japan Must Fight Piracy, Ex-Defense Chief Says." *Bloomberg.com* (15 January 2009), http://www.bloomberg.com/apps/news?pid=20601101&sid=a6PZ5sr9KacA&refer=japan (accessed 16 January 2009).

Saul, Jonathan. "Planes Seen as Crucial against Somali Piracy." *Reuters* (28 April 2009), http://www.reuters.com/article/worldNews/idUSTRE53R4LX20090428 (accessed 8 May 2009).

Schaub, Gary. "Really Soft Power." *The New York Times*, 27 January 2009, A29.

Schmitt, John F. "A Systemic Concept for Operational Design." 2006.

Shanker, Thom. "U.S. Urges Merchant Ships to Try Steps to Foil Pirates." *The New York Times* (20 November 2008), http://www.nytimes.com/2008/11/20/washington/20military.html?_r=2.

Sizemore, Bill. "Sailors on Blackwater Anti-Piracy Ship Claim Harassment." In *The Virginian-Pilot*. Place Published, 14 May 2009.

Smyth, Jamie. "EU Agrees on Mission to Combat Piracy." *The Irish Times*, 3 October 2008.

Spiegel, Peter. "Bush Administration Had Issued Plans for Pirates in December." *The Wall Street Journal*, 9 April 2009, A8.

Stolberg, Sheryl Gay. "On First Day, Obama Quickly Sets a New Tone." *The New York Times*, 21 January 2009, A1.

Tugwell, Paul. "Shipping Unites in 'Crisis Call'." *Lloyd's List*, 19 September 2008, 1.

Viscusi, Gregory. "Pirate Attacks Cut Dramatically by Navies, US Admiral Says." *Bloomberg.com* (27 January 2009), http://www.bloomberg.com/apps/news?pid=20601102&sid=aXR8.j52hcpo&refer=uk (accessed 28 January 2009).

Waltz, Kenneth N. "Structural Realism after the Cold War." *International Security* 25, no. 1 (Summer 2000): 5–41.

Watkins, Eric. "Pirates Seize Another Tanker Off Yemen." *Oil and Gas Journal* (9 January 2009), http://www.ogj.com/display_article/352052/7/ONART/none/Trasp/1/Pirates-seize-another-tanker-off-Yemen/ (accessed 9 January 2009).

Weiser, Benjamin. "Pirate Suspect Charged as Adult in New York." *The New York Times*, 22 April 2009, A1.

Wilson, Brian, and James Kraska. "Anti-Piracy Patrols Presage Rising Naval Powers." *YaleGlobal* (13 January 2009), http://yaleglobal.yale.edu/display.article?id=11808 (accessed 11 February 2009).

Wood, I.D.H. "Piracy Is Deadlier Than Ever." *United States Naval Institute Proceedings* 126, no. 1 (January 2000): 60–63.

Yerak, Becky. "Arrr! Aon Hoists Insurance against Pirates." *Chicago Tribune* (13 January 2009), http://www.chicagotribune.com/business/chi-biz-aon-pirate-insurance-jan13,0,5871065.story (accessed 13 January 2009).

Yost, Mark. "Whos, Whats, Wheres of the Whydah." *The Wall Street Journal* (1 April 2009), http://online.wsj.com/article/SB123862751510180275.html (accessed 3 April 2009).

Zakaria, Fareed. "This Isn't the Return of History." *Newsweek*, 8 September 2008, 63.

Books

"Freeboard." In *Merriam-Webster's Collegiate Dictionary* Springfield, MA: Merriam-Webster, Inc., 2003.

Anderson, Fred, and Andrew Cayton. *The Dominion of War: Empire and Liberty in North America 1500–2000*. New York: Penguin Group, 2005.

Andrews, Kenneth R. *Elizabethan Privateering: English Privateering During the Spanish War, 1585–1603*. Cambridge: Cambridge University Press, 1964.

Art, Robert J. "The Strategy of Selective Engagement." In *The Use of Force: Military Power and International Politics*, edited by Robert J. Art and Kenneth N. Waltz. Lanham, MD: Rowman and Littlefield Publishers, Inc., 2004.

Baldwin, David A. *Economic Statecraft*. Princeton: Princeton University Press, 1985.

Barlow, Jeffrey G. *Revolt of the Admirals: The Fight for Naval Aviation 1945–1950*. Washington, DC: Government Reprints Press, 2001.

Bass, George Fletcher. *A History of Seafaring: Based on Underwater Archaeology*. London: Thames and Hudson, 1972.

Berger, Thomas U. *Cultures of Antimilitarism: National Security in Germany and Japan*. Baltimore, MD: Johns Hopkins University Press, 1998.

Bishop, Morris. *The Middle Ages*. Illustrated ed. Boston, MA: Houghton Mifflin Harcourt, 2001.

Braund, Susanna Morton. "Praise and Protreptic in Early Imperial Panegyric: Cicero, Seneca, Pliny." In *The Propaganda of Power: The Role of Panegyric in Late Antiquity*, edited by Mary Whitby, 53–76. Leiden: Brill, 1998.

Brown, Michael E. "Security Problems and Security Policy in a Grave New World." In *Grave New World: Security Challenges in the 21st Century*, edited by Michael E. Brown. Washington, DC: Georgetown University Press, 2003.

Burnett, John S. *Dangerous Waters: Modern Piracy and Terror on the High Seas*. New York: Penguin Putnam, Inc., 2002.

Carse, Robert. *The Age of Piracy: A History*. New York: Rinehart and Company, Inc., 1957.

Clausewitz, Carl von. *On War*. Translated by Michael Eliot Howard and Peter Paret. Edited by Michael Eliot Howard and Peter Paret. Revised ed. Princeton, NJ: Princeton University Press, 1984.

Cohen, Eliot A. *Supreme Command: Soldiers, Statesmen, and Leadership in Wartime*. 2003 ed. New York: Anchor Books, 2002.

Corbett, Julian Stafford. *Some Principles of Maritime Strategy*. Annapolis, MD: United States Naval Institute, 1988.

De Souza, Philip. *Piracy in the Graeco-Roman World*. Cambridge: Cambridge University Press, 2002.

Dobbins, James, Seth G. Jones, Keith Crane, and Beth Cole DeGrasse. *The Beginner's Guide to Nation-Building*. Santa Monica, CA: The RAND Corporation, 2007.

Duffield, John S. *World Power Forsaken: Political Culture, International Institutions, and German Security Policy after Unification*. Stanford, CA: Stanford University Press, 1998.

Eltis, David. *Economic Growth and the Ending of the Transatlantic Slave Trade*. Illustrated ed. Oxford: Oxford University Press, 1987.

Gaĭduk, Ilya V. *The Great Confrontation: Europe and Islam through the Centuries*. Chicago: Ivan R. Dee, 2003.

Gosse, Philip. *The History of Piracy*. Tudor ed. New York: Longmans, Green and Co., 1932.

Gottschalk, Jack A., and Brian P. Flanagan. *Jolly Roger with an Uzi: The Rise and Threat of Modern Piracy*. Annapolis, MD: Naval Institute Press, 2000.

Graham-Campbell, James, and David M. (FRW) Wilson. *The Viking World*. Third ed. London: Frances Lincoln, Ltd., 2001.

Gray, Colin S. *Explorations in Strategy*. Westport, CT: Praeger, 1996.

———. *Fighting Talk: Forty Maxims on War, Peace, and Strategy*. Westport, CT: Praeger Security International, 2007.

———. *Modern Strategy*. Oxford: Oxford University Press, 1999.

Greenburg, Michael D., Peter Chalk, Henry H. Willis, Ivan Khilko, and David S. Ortiz. *Maritime Terrorism: Risk and Liability*. Santa Monica, CA: RAND Corporation, 2006.

Heilbroner, Robert, and Lester Thurow. *Economics Explained: Everything You Need to Know About How the Economy Works and Where It's Going*. 1998 ed. New York: Touchstone, 1982.

Huntington, Samuel P. *The Soldier and the State: The Theory of Politics and Civil-Military Relations*. 1985 ed. Cambridge, MA: The Belknap Press of Harvard University Press, 1957.

Janis, Irving L. *Groupthink: Psychological Studies of Policy Decisions and Fiascoes*. Second ed. Boston: Houghton Mifflin, 1982.

Jervis, Robert. *System Effects: Complexity in Political and Social Life*. Princeton NJ: Princeton University Press, 1997.

Johnston, Alastair Iain. *Cultural Realism: Strategic Culture and Grand Strategy in Chinese History*. Princeton: Princeton University Press, 1995.

Kaplan, Fred. *Daydream Believers: How a Few Grand Ideas Wrecked American Power*. Hoboken, NJ: John Wiley and Sons, Inc., 2008.

Kissinger, Henry. *Diplomacy*. New York: Simon & Schuster Paperbacks, 1994.

———. "An End of Hubris." In *The World in 2009*, 46. London: The Economist, December 2008.

Konstam, Angus. *Piracy: The Complete History*. Oxford: Osprey Publishing, 2008.

Lapid, Yosef. "Culture's Ship: Returns and Departures in International Relations Theory." In *The Return of Culture and Identity in IR Theory*, edited by Yosef Lapid and Friedrich Kratochwil. Boulder, CO: Lynne Rienner, 1996.

LaRochelle, Dennis M., Jack A. Gottschalk, and Brian P. Flanagan. "The Economic Cost." In *Jolly Roger with an Uzi*, 85–108. Annapolis, MD: Naval Institute Press, 2000.

Liddell, Henry George, and Robert Scott. "Peirates." In *A Greek-English Lexicon*, edited by Henry Stuart Jones. Oxford: Clarendon Press, 1940.

Macmillan, Alan, and Ken Booth. "Appendix: Strategic Culture–Framework for Analysis." In *Strategic Cultures in the Asia-Pacific Region*, edited by Ken Booth and Russell Trood. New York: St. Martin's Press, 1999.

Mahan, Alfred Thayer. *The Influence of Sea Power Upon History, 1660–1783*. Boston: Little, Brown, and Company, 1918.

Marley, David. *Pirates and Privateers of the Americas*. Santa Barbara, CA: ABC-CLIO, 1994.

McNeill, William H. *The Pursuit of Power: Technology, Armed Force, and Society since AD 1000*. Chicago: The University of Chicago Press, 1982.

Moran, Theodore H. "Defense Economics and Security." In *Grave New World: Security Challenges in the 21st Century*, edited by Michael E. Brown, 133–56. Washington, DC: Georgetown University Press, 2003.

Myers, David J. "Threat Perception and Strategic Response of the Regional Hegemons: A Conceptual Overview." In *Regional Hegemons: Threat Perception and Strategic Response*, edited by David J. Myers, 1–29. Boulder, CO: Westview Press, Inc., 1991.

Naylor, R.T. *Wages of Crime: Black Markets, Illegal Finance, and the Underworld Economy*. Ithaca, NY: Cornell University Press, 2002.

Niou, Emerson M.S., Peter C. Ordeshook, and Gregory F. Rose. *The Balance of Power: Stability in International Systems*. Cambridge: Cambridge University Press, 1989.

Nye, Joseph S. *Soft Power: The Means to Success in World Politics*. Cambridge, MA: Perseus Books Group, 2004.

Olson, Mancur. *The Logic of Collective Action: Public Goods and the Theory of Groups*. 1971 ed. Cambridge, MA: Harvard University Press, 1965.

Plutarch. *Plutarch's Lives of Coriolanus, Caesar, Brutus, and Antonius*. Translated by Thomas North and R.H. Carr. Oxford: Clarendon Press, 1906.

———. *Roman Lives*. Translated by Robin Waterfield. Oxford: Oxford University Press, 1999.

Riker, William H. *The Art of Political Manipulation*. New Haven, CT: Yale University Press, 1986.

Robinson, William Morrison, Jr. *The Confederate Privateers*. New Haven, CT: Yale University Press, 1928.

Rogoziński, Jan. *Honor among Thieves: Captain Kidd, Henry Every, and the Pirate Democracy in the Indian Ocean*. Mechanicsburg, PA: Stackpole Books, 2000.

Rosecrance, Richard N. *Action and Reaction in World Politics*. Boston: Little, Brown Co., 1963.

Schelling, Thomas C. *Arms and Influence*. New Haven, CT: Yale University Press, 1966.

Sloan, Geoffrey, and Colin S. Gray. *Geopolitics, Geography and Strategy*. Illustrated ed. New York: Routledge, 1999.

Strang, Gilbert. *Introduction to Applied Mathematics*. Cambridge, MA: Wellesley-Cambridge Press, 1986.

Thucydides. *The Landmark Thucydides: A Comprehensive Guide to the Peloponnesian War*. Translated by Richard Crawley. Edited by Robert B. Strassler. 1st Touchstone ed. New York, NY: Simon & Schuster, 1998.

Waltz, Kenneth N. *Theory of International Politics*. New York: McGraw-Hill, Inc., 1979.

Walzer, Michael. *Just and Unjust Wars: A Moral Argument with Historical Illustrations*. 4th ed. New York: BasicBooks, 2006.

White, Leslie A. *The Concept of Cultural Systems: A Key to Understanding Tribes and Nations*. New York: Columbia University Press, 1975.

Government Documents

US Congress. Senate. Armed Services Committee. *Armed Services Committee Hearing on Piracy*, 111th Cong., 1st sess., 5 May 2009.

"A Cooperative Strategy for 21st Century Seapower." US Navy, US Marine Corps, and US Coast Guard, October 2007.

"Quadrennial Roles and Missions Review Report." Washington, DC: Department of Defense, January 2009.

"Taking Diplomatic Action against Piracy." Bureau of Public Affairs: US Department of State, 13 May 2009.

"United Nations Convention on the Law of the Sea." Division for Ocean Affairs and the Law of the Sea: United Nations, 10 December 1982.

Commander, US Fifth Fleet. "Combined Task Force 150." *US Naval Forces Central Command* (8 April 2009), http://www.cusnc.navy.mil/command/ctf150.html (accessed 8 April 2009).

———. "Combined Task Force 151." *US Naval Forces Central Command* (8 April 2009), http://www.cusnc.navy.mil/command/ctf150.html (accessed 8 April 2009).

———. "Combined Task Force 152." *US Naval Forces Central Command* (8 April 2009), http://www.cusnc.navy.mil/command/ctf150.html (accessed 8 April 2009).

McCreary, John. "NightWatch." AFCEA Intelligence, 29 January 2009.

US Congress. Senate. Committee on Foreign Relations. *Militarization of Foreign Policy: Hearing before the Committee on Foreign Relations*, 110th Congress, 2nd sess., 31 July 2008.

Ridenour, C.H. "Methods of Bombing Shipping Targets." Headquarters Seventh Fighter Wing, 20 February 1943.

Personal Communications

Chalk, Peter. (RAND Corporation), interview by author, 30 January 2009.

Ferdinand, Kevin. (Major, Royal Canadian Air Force), in discussion with the author, 6 November 2008.

Linardi, Anthony J. (Commander, US Navy), in discussion with the author, 12 November 2008.

———. (Commander, US Navy), in discussion with the author, 2 April 2009.

McKnight, Terry. (Rear Admiral, US Navy; Commander, Task Force 151), Interview: Department of Defense Bloggers' Roundtable, 29 January 2009.

Shipping message. (First Engineer, *Maersk Alabama*), in electronic mail to *Maersk Arkansas* First Engineer, 10 April 2009.

Stilwell, Eric L. (Captain, US Navy), in discussion with the author, 19 November 2008.

Reports (no author listed)

"1997 Annual Report on Piracy and Armed Robbery against Ships." Kuala Lumpur: International Maritime Bureau, 31 March 1998.

"2004 Annual Report on Piracy and Armed Robbery against Ships." Kuala Lumpur: International Maritime Bureau, 31 January 2005.

"2006 Annual Report on Piracy and Armed Robbery against Ships." Kuala Lumpur: International Maritime Board, 31 January 2007.

"2007 Annual Report on Piracy and Armed Robbery against Ships." Kuala Lumpur: International Maritime Board, 31 January 2008.

"2008 Annual Report on Piracy and Armed Robbery against Ships." Kuala Lumpur: International Maritime Bureau, 31 January 2009.

"United Nations Convention on the Law of the Sea." United Nations Division for Ocean Affairs and the Law of the Sea, 10 December 1982.

"UNSC Resolution 1851." edited by United Nations Security Council, 16 December 2008.

Reports (author or authors listed)

Bruyneel, M. "Current Reports on Piracy by the IMO and the IMB—a Comparison." Amsterdam: Center for Maritime Research (MARE) and International Institute for Asian Studies (IIAS), 4 September 2003.

Chalk, Peter. "The Maritime Dimension of International Security: Terrorism, Piracy and Challenges for the United States." In *Project Air Force*. Santa Monica, CA: RAND, 2008.

Commercial Crime Services. "Live Piracy Site." International Chamber of Commerce (http://www.ics-ccs.org), 2009.

International Maritime Board. "Live Piracy Map." London: International Chamber of Commerce, 2009.

———. "Piracy Map 2005." London: International Chamber of Commerce, 2005.

———. "Piracy Map 2006." London: International Chamber of Commerce, 2006.

———. "Piracy Map 2007." London: International Chamber of Commerce, 2007.

Junker, Karin, Michel-Ange Scarbonchi, and Fodé Sylla. "Report of the Ad Hoc Delegation of the CDC on Its Mission to Djibouti." Brussels: European Parliament, 2004.

Naval Studies Board. "Autonomous Vehicles in Support of Naval Operations." Washington, DC: National Research Council, 2005.

———. "C4ISR for Future Naval Strike Groups." Washington, DC: National Research Council, 2006.

Rosen, Stephen Peter, and Aaron Friedberg. "Strategies for Long-Term Competition with China." Washington, DC: Office of the Secretary of Defense/Net Assessment, 2008.

Snyder, Jack. "The Soviet Strategic Culture: Implications for Nuclear Options." Santa Monica, CA: RAND Corporation, 1977.

www.ingramcontent.com/pod-product-compliance
Lightning Source LLC
Chambersburg PA
CBHW052003280526
45793CB00005B/833